The Snake Almanac

The Snake Almanac

A Fully Illustrated Natural History of Snakes Worldwide

Edward R. Ricciuti

The Lyons Press

To the Stricklers, my neighbors across the swamp

CONTENTS

CONTENTS

ACKNOWLEDGMENTS

I wish to express my thanks to Steve Berube and Linda Krulikowski for their special help on this book. I was truly lucky to have Steve as the illustrator because he has studied at the Lyme Academy of Fine Arts in Old Lyme, Connecticut, is an expert and a lecturer on snakes, and has an academic background in ecology and evolutionary biology. Linda, who took the majority of photographs, also lectures on snakes and has photographed some of the most venomous snakes in the world. Many of her photographs have required daring, because she does not use a telephoto lens but records their images up close and personal, sometimes creeping up to rattlesnakes and snapping their pictures literally face to face.

INTRODUCTION

Friend or Foe?

Once, longer ago than I like to admit, I regarded snakes as my foes. The year was 1948. I was 10 years of age, and welling up in my juvenile soul was an interest in wild creatures that would eventually lead me to working as a zoological society curator and a writer-naturalist. My family had moved into a new home, in a development at the semi-rural fringes of a fading industrial city; Waterbury, Connecticut. The field adjoining our small plot of property was still hayed with a team of horses. Within a few years, the rural façade would disappear and the neighborhood would become one of cheek-by-jowl homes.

A sign of things to come was what had happened to the small brook that ran through our yard. It had been a meandering meadow stream but then was channelized by a developer. My father had shored up its artificial banks with stone walls. As it usually happens when a stream is ditched, its ability to support flora and fauna is greatly diminished. Nevertheless, the water of the brook still housed a handful of wild creatures, although they were dwindling, if not doomed. Caddis fly larvae clung to the undersides of rocks. In the few pools, a handful of small fish—black-nosed dace—darted about. Here and there were frogs. Shoeless, I explored the brook, poking around to find its inhabitants. One of the creatures that lived there, I discovered, was a relatively large snake, about a yard long, with a body as thick as a knockwurst sausage. Its skin was reddish brown, with a pattern of dark blotches. "Yikes," I thought. "It's a water moccasin." I erred, as many Northeasterners who do not read reptile field books still do, by mistaking the non-venomous northern water snake for a highly venomous serpent, also called the "cottonmouth," which lives no farther north than southeast Virginia.

The water snake hissed at me. Although not venomous, northern water snakes aggressively respond to danger. They are prone to bite, the result of which may cause serious bleeding because of an anticoagulant in their saliva. Of course, I didn't know this at the time, nor did I realize that had it been a cottonmouth, I might have been dead meat. I was carrying a large stick, to help me navigate slippery rocks. I bravely jabbed it at the snake. It struck at me and, fortunately for me, barely pricked my arm. I ran like blazes and vowed thereafter not to bother the serpent again. I saw it a few more times in subsequent weeks, but gave it a wide berth. And, when I considered the snake's courage—after all, even as a 10-year-old, I towered over it like a *T. Rex* over a little lizard—I grew to admire it.

In the years that followed, I learned to view snakes as friends rather than foes. I encountered them often in the wild and in captivity. I became fascinated with their physiology and behavior, their quirks and adaptations, their beauty (many snakes are as colorful as the most stunning birds), the aura of raw power in some species, and the fragility of others.

Of all my encounters with snakes in the wild, the one that I remember most is meeting a forest cobra in Kenya. The forest cobra is a sizeable snake, averaging about six to seven feet long, and heavy of body, as cobras go. It is not known to be aggressive, but its bite packs a wallop of venom that can be potentially fatal to a human.

It was 1973, and I was on the first of what would be many assignments in Africa. I was driving a compact Datsun sedan—

it proved able to handle rough dirt roads with ease—down a rutted track through the bush. I drove slowly, not wanting to break an axle in the myriad potholes. Thus, I was able to spy a shape, glossy black and as thick as the bicep of an NFL lineman, stretched halfway across the roadway. It was a snake, its rear hidden in brush to the left side of the road, its fore in the middle of the track. I eased the vehicle to a halt within a yard or so of the animal and opened the window to get a clear look at the creature. As soon as I poked my head out of the open window, the snake somehow sensed it. The cobra erupted into action. In a flash, it emitted a hissing, mighty expulsion of air, which sounded like the breaking of a steam pipe, and launched itself a good two feet across the ground. The entire length of its body catapulted into the bush on my right. Then, it disappeared.

The instantaneous reaction of the snake, its lightning move for a creature of its size, and the mighty sound it made, audible to me in the vehicle, left an indelible impression in my memory.

There have been periods in my life during which several non-venomous snakes, ranging in size from an 18-inch corn snake to a nine-foot boa constrictor, resided in our home. I kept them in cages, of course, although they often were let out to be handled and, in the case of a memorable five-foot indigo snake, to exercise by snaking—no pun—across the kitchen floor. None of these snakes had been purchased from a dealer. All were given to me. Some came from people who had kept them as pets but had eventually grown tired of them. Others came from organizations and institutions that considered them as surplus.

My children, two daughters and a son, now fully grown, grew up with snakes in their home. They saw them feed on mice and rats. They learned the proper way to pick up and hold a snake. And they learned the identifying marks of various species. And I learned that when one teaches youngsters not to fear snakes, or other wild animals for that matter, they also need to develop a healthy respect for the fact that some snakes can be dangerous and even deadly. The boa constrictor that my daughters regularly touched without incident viciously bit a keeper at a zoo where I had placed him on exhibit loan. The keeper, new and unfamiliar with handling snakes, had made a quick grab at the boa and tried to yank it out of a corner in the exhibit. He startled the snake and was nailed in the arm. When I told my daughters what had happened, they could not believe that "our" snake had bitten someone. When handling snakes, I replied, it pays to be very, very gentle.

Apparently, I allowed my son, our youngest child, to become overly familiar with snakes. He had been around them almost from day one. To him, they were as much a part of the household as our dog and cats. When he was still a toddler, we moved from a suburban Connecticut town to one that was relatively rural. Shortly thereafter, while he and I were out back of the house, I saw him looking at a small snake, which was within reach of his small arms. I saw that he was about to try to pick up the creature, so I quickly went over to him. Wise move on my part. At the tip of the snake's tail was a "button," the beginning of a growth that would become a rattle. I picked up the little timber rattlesnake with a stick and released it into my woods—hoping that I would not unexpectedly encounter it when it grew up.

Why did I not kill the baby rattler? It was not because I am adverse to killing animals. I have raised animals for food. I hunt and fish. But I do not kill any creature indiscriminately and have worked hard to encourage support for imperiled species. Timber rattlers are endangered in my state and protected by law. Unlike the whitetail deer or the wild turkey, timber rattlesnakes are dwindling as a species. If their kind is to survive, every one of them counts. The disappearance of any species, animal or plant, impoverishes and even threatens our world. Would we be better off without breeds of mosquitoes that spread fatal diseases? That is a tough question, indeed. It is very difficult to know where to draw the line. Perhaps I should have dispatched the little rattler. But there were more than 100 acres of woodland out in back, so I figured I could give the baby snake some space.

It is much more difficult to engender sympathy for dwindling species of snakes than for whales or elephants. Fear and loathing of snakes seems almost inbred in many people, especially in Western societies—certainly due in part to the Biblical image of the serpent as the Devil incarnate. I know people who shoot snakes on sight. A woman acquaintance of mine has such a phobia about these reptiles that I saw her faint at the sight of a little garter snake. Over the years, I have tried to educate people about snakes. I have brought them to lectures at schools and clubs, and have taken them on television programs. I have found that with proper presentation, fear of snakes can be turned into fascination or, at least, an understanding of these creatures. Many years ago, I taught religious education on Sunday mornings to grade schoolers at my Roman Catholic parish. My course was the Old Testament and it would include a discussion of imagery in the Bible. Given the difficulty of explaining this topic to kids who would undoubtedly watch the clock instead of listening to me, I decided to hook them on the first day of class. I introduced myself and then produced a large sack. "The Devil is in it," I told the children. Some snickered or chuckled. Others rolled their eyes. I opened the sack and produced my boa constrictor. It definitely got their attention. After the class calmed down, I offered my opinion that, to the writers of the Old Testament, the serpent may have been a fearful creature, so it became symbolic of the Tempter who caused the downfall of Adam and Eve. Whether or not my theology was on target, I believe that I converted a bunch of youngsters to the support of snakes. Most of my students remained after class, looking at the snake, touching it, and asking questions. I left class thinking that I had taught them something about their religion, but had also given them insight into conservation of nature, which can be a religion of itself.

Just as I had done when I was a boy, many people view snakes as foes. It escapes many people that the vast majority of snakes are not venomous and present no danger to humans. Of course, a few non-venomous snakes, notably some of the larger constrictors, such as the anaconda and python, are potentially dangerous, but usually under situations that are quite out of the ordinary. I never mask the fact that some snakes can be dangerous and, indeed, deadly, but more people in the United States are injured or killed by pet pooches than by snakes. Admittedly, the same cannot be said for some other parts of the world.

Like so many other wild animals, snakes are more threatened by our species than we are by them. By and large, destruction of habitat is the main threat to these animals. The trade in snake skin, used for items such as boots and purses, has also contributed to the decrease in some species. So has the pet trade, although legitimate dealers do not conduct commerce in snakes that are protected by law.

Even those who have an aversion for snakes have a practical reason for helping them prosper. Many snakes feed largely on rodents, such as rats and mice. They are a natural control on these animals, keeping populations balanced. Snakes, moreover, provide food for other animals, such as birds of prey. Were it not for snakes, lurking in hidden places, crawling on their bellies over the ground, hawks and eagles, rulers of the sky, might find their world diminished, as would we.

The Snake Almanac

Late Arrivals

Although snakes have a primeval image in the minds of many people, they are late arrivals upon the evolutionary scene, at least as far as reptiles are concerned. Snakes did not evolve until long after most other major groups of reptiles, both species that are extant and those that became extinct, were firmly established. Snakes arose from lizards, which emerged upon the world's stage as the so-called "Age of Dinosaurs" was ticking towards its end. As far as the fossil record is concerned, the first snakes date back some 90 millon years, about 30 million years before the last dinosaurs went into oblivion. Some recent evidence suggests that snakes may be somewhat older, but even so, they are thoroughly modern reptiles. Thus far, in fact, they are the evolutionary culmination of the reptilian class.

There are four orders of living reptiles. The tuatara of New Zealand, a lizard-like creature with a light-sensitive pit in its forehead that amounts to a "third eye," is the only living member of its order, Rhynchocephalia, also known as Sphenodontia.

The other orders are the turtles (Order *Chelonia*), the crocodilians (*Crocodylia*) and the Squamates, lizards and snakes (*Squamata*).

To understand the position of snakes in the evolutionary order of things, one must consider the evolution of the entire class of reptiles. The first reptiles arose from amphibian ancestors about 250 million years ago. Not until 150 million years later would snakes inhabit our planet. Ironically, perhaps, many early reptiles had traces of mammalian characteristics. Some of them were, in fact, ancestors of the mammals. Indeed, millions of years before snakes made their appearance, birds were flying and small, rat-size mammals were furtively scurrying through the night, a tactic that helped them avoid the lightweights of the dinosaur clan that might be tempted to snack upon them. Many species of dinosaurs had vanished long before the lizards made their entrance upon the world scene. The time frame in which lizards and snakes fit into the geologic history of Earth is evident from the following chart describing key events in the evolution of life. This chart is only representative, providing some of the significant life forms and when the fossil record—by no means perfect—indicates they appeared.

Time	*Life Forms*
Precambrian Eras 2.5 billion–540 million years ago (mya)	Blue-green algae, coelenterates, primitive worms
PALEOZOIC ERA	
Cambrian Period 540–505 mya	Trilobites, mollusks and many other aquatic invertebrates
Ordovician Period 505–438 mya	Armored jawless fishes appear, mollusks and squid-like cephalopods prosper

Time	Life Forms
Silurian Period 438–408 mya	Jawless fishes increase, scorpions and other arthropods appear, corals
Devonian Period 408–360 mya	Spiders, the first insects, and bony fishes; amphibians evolve from bony fishes
Carboniferous Period 360–286 mya	Flying insects, the first reptiles; some reptiles begin to develop mammal-like features sharks abundant, tree ferns
Permian Period 286–245 mya	Mammal-like reptiles abound and radiate, insects proliferate, trilobites vanish, conifers appear

MESOZOIC ERA

Triassic Period 245–208 mya	The first dinosaurs, small in size; turtles, proto-crocodilians; reptiles give rise to the first primitive mammals
Jurassic Period 208–144 mya	Dinosaurs abound, with classic animals such as apatosaurs, allosaurs and stegosaurs. Mammals, still small, begin to proliferate; the first birds; pterosaurs, the flying reptiles.

Time	Life Forms
Cretaceous Period	The most advanced dinosaurs, including *T. Rex* and *Triceratops.* In terms of evolutionary advancement, if not in variety, the Cretaceous was the zenith of the dinosaurs and the downfall of the dinosaurs. When this period was ended, the dinosaurs were gone. The Age of Reptiles, called the Mesozoic, was over. Perhaps in the wake of the dinosaurs, the turtles and crocodilians remained. And, as the dinosaurs were fading, lizards appeared and soon gave rise to snakes.
CENOZOIC ERA **TERTIARY PERIOD**	
Paleocene Eocene Epoch 66.4–36.6 mya	Modern bivalves, such as clams; mammals increase; snakes begin to expand in terms of species and geography. Precursors of modern mammals begin to evolve. Snakes continue to diversify.
Oligocene Epoch 36.6–23.7 mya	Modern mammals, such as bats, apes, cats, dogs and horses continue to evolve.

Time	Life Forms
Miocene Epoch 23.7–5.3 mya	Mammals approach their greatest diversity; saber-toothed cats, horses, apes and the lineage leading to humans diverge.
Pliocene Epoch 5.3–1.6 mya	Mammals approach truly modern forms. Homonids evolving.
Pleistocene Epoch 1.6–million—10,000 years ago	Homonids produce modern humans. Giant bison, mammoths, cave bears and many other members of the Ice-Age fauna disappear. Modern groups of snakes well established.
Recent	Some snakes imperiled or vanished due to human activities.

Legless Lizards?

Trivia question: what is the difference between a snake and a lizard? The obvious answer might seem to be that lizards have legs and snakes do not. Obvious, perhaps, but not entirely correct.

Some of the first snakes may well have had legs. In March, 2000, a paper in the journal *Science* published a report by a team of researchers from the Field Museum in Chicago about a fossil snake—that had *legs*. Admittedly, the legs were mere stumps, but they were legs, indeed. And therein lies a tale.

The fossil, which goes by the scientific name *Hassiophis terrasanctus*, had been sitting in a drawer within the Hebrew University in Jerusalem since the early 1980s, where its discoverer, Georg Haas, had placed it—and perhaps—forgotten it. Researchers from Field, led by Oliver Rieppel, tracked down the fossil and examined it. The projections were small but, in the eyes of the researchers, qualified as legs—not used for locomotion but, perhaps during the mating processes, for clasping squirmy bodies together.

Some of the more primitive living snakes, such as the boids, have hints of hind leg bones in their skeletons. They retain the vestigial remains of a pelvis, essential for supporting rear limbs. And some of them have small spurs that project out of the body from the vestigial pelvis, which, like the legs of the fossil described above, are thought to aid in mating.

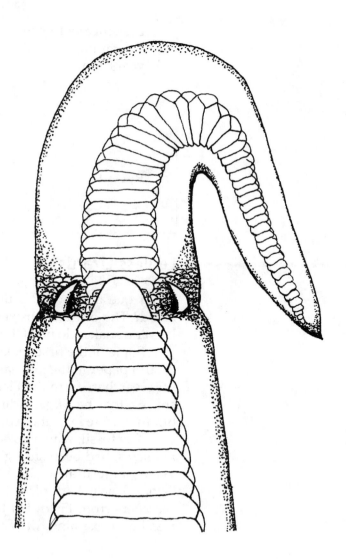

The primitive nature of boa constrictors is evidenced by the tiny spurs at the rear of the body. Vestigial remnants of legs inherited from lizard ancestors, these spurs are used for clasping when boas mate.

On the other side of the coin, several types of lizards are legless. The glass lizard, which inhabits the southeastern and midwestern United States, looks exactly like a snake, slender and up to almost four feet in length. This lizard's short tail, indistinguishable to the lay person's eye from its much longer body, breaks into pieces if grabbed, allowing the lizard to escape and giving rise to its name. The tail regenerates if the lizard survives. As the glass lizard illustrates, the presence or absence of legs is not always indicative of whether or not a reptile is a snake or a lizard.

Another general difference is the fact that the eyes of snakes remain forever open because their eyelids cannot move. Most—there is that word "most" again—lizards can close their eyes.

But, perhaps the one feature that truly distinguishes snakes from lizards lies in the ears, or lack of them. Lizards have an external ear opening and an eardrum. They hear sounds that are carried as pressure waves through the air, the way humans hear as well. Snakes do not have an external ear opening or eardrum. Thus, they do not "hear" the way humans and lizards do. Instead of sensing sound waves disturbing the air, they sense vibrations passing through solid matter and, in the case of aquatic snakes, water. In terms of survival, this ability is a signal advantage. After all, a snake lives virtually all of its life in close contact—literally belly-to-belly—with a substrate, be it the ground or a tree limb.

The snake senses vibrations through bones in its lower jaw. The joint of a reptile's jaw is created by the joining of two bones, the articular and the quadrate. Vibrations enter the quadrate bone and move through the articular, from which they travel to the inner ear. From there, the process is similar to that of most other vertebrates. The vibrations are sent to the brain, which receives them as sensory messages.

Despite these differences, most scientists who study reptiles consider snakes as lizards, albeit lizards with a highly specialized lifestyle. Following is a chart showing the classification of reptiles, including snakes, which most taxonomists now except. But beware. Taxonomists, scientists who classify animals according to evolutionary relationships, continually refine and alter their opinions of how different groups of animals and, indeed, species, are related. When it comes to taxonomy, the times, and the family trees, are always sprouting new branches. The accepted taxonomy of today may well be anathema tomorrow.

THE FAMILY TREE OF SNAKES AND LIZARDS

Phylum: Chordata (chordates): Animals having, at some stage of their development, a dorsal tubular nerve chord.

Subphylum: Vertebrata (vertebrates): Animals with backbones, or spinal columns, of bone or cartilage.

Class: Reptilia (reptiles): Cold-blooded, air-breathing vertebrates, usually having a scaly or plated covering.

Subclass: Lepidsauria (lepidosaurians): Animals with scales.

Order: Squamata (squamates): Reptiles posessing scales but not ossifications in the skin.

Suborder Serpentes aka Ophidia (serpents)

Enter the Serpent

At one unknown point during the middle of the Cretaceous period when dinosaurs still ruled and flowering plants began to bloom across the land, the creature that we know as a snake was added to the list of the Earth's fauna. Like their descendants, the early snakes fed strictly on animal matter. As far as scientists know, there never has been a vegetarian snake.

Snakes worked their way over the ground and, judging from fossil evidence, into the trees as well. What did they hunt? Probably primitive birds and mammals, insects and other invertebrates. And possibly other reptiles—reptiles were the most abundant vertebrates, so it makes sense that the early snakes might focus upon them.

Scientists are not sure of the lizard lineage that produced snakes. It could have been the Varanid lizards, more commonly called "monitors," active, with low-slung bodies, and relentless hunters. Among these fierce predators is the Komodo monitor, the world's largest lizard, which can grow more than 10 feet long and weigh almost 300 pounds, as much as a medium-size lion. Deer, wild pigs, goats and, on rare occasion, people, are its prey. Like snakes, monitor lizards have a forked tongue. That fact is not enough to link the two groups, but there is a strong scientific suspicion that the monitors, or something like them, may be the progenitors of serpents.

The head profile of monitor lizards (shown on top) is very similar to that of many snakes, in this case a vine snake (bottom). Monitors may be close to the lizard progenitors of serpents.

The visages of the first snakes are lost in time. They are known to science only by a few bones, largely vertebrae that, lucky for us, were fossilized. What did they look like? What did they do? It is impossible to accurately picture a creature that has been extinct for millions of years from a few bone fragments. Scientists have tried and often failed. The behavior of ancient snakes is lost in time. They probably lived much as their modern descendants do. They may have coiled into humus created by the leaves of the first deciduous trees. They may have worked their way high into tree ferns, elder plants, ancient when the first flower blossomed. Before too long, geologically speaking, dinosaurs (except for birds, which are viewed by many scientists as "feathered dinosaurs,") were gone. Their demise may have been due to a cosmic collision (the now-fashionable theory), or a change of climate. Whatever the reason, the dinosaurs gave up the crown as ruling reptiles and, indeed, kings of the land, and vanished. The snakes, as well as their lizard kin, were waiting in the wings along with primitive mammals. With the passing of the dinosaurs, they flourished.

11

Ironically, some of the earliest groups of serpents that survived the dinosaurs are still common today. These are the boids, typified among living snakes by the boa constrictor and anaconda. (Some scientists regard pythons as members of the same group. Other researchers consider pythons as a separate family due to differences in reproductive methods and geographic distribution.) The fact that boids—as well as pythons—have nubs of rear leg bones in their skeleton, are evident as small spurs near the vent, while most other snakes do not, testify to their antiquity. So do their teeth, which are not specialized for cutting-edge techniques such as venom injection. From a layman's standpoint, the backward-curved teeth of a boa constrictor resemble those of a Komodo monitor. These teeth are used for grabbing flesh of prey and bolting it down. The monitor, however, cuts up its victim and swallows chunks of flesh. Snakes gulp down the meal whole. Reptiles, as a group, do not chew as mammals do. That, in fact, is a major evolutionary difference between reptiles and mammals. The more advanced dentition of mammals enables them to chew food and break it down before the inside juices continue the work. Reptiles, as a group, do not chew. They bolt their food. The ability to chew is a major evolutionary difference between reptiles and mammals. Chewing food increases its energy efficiency, which has helped mammals gain their ascendency as the Earth's latest ruling creatures. Chewing also liberates chemicals that trigger the action of taste buds.

Boids prospered in the Eocene epoch, which was once popularly called the "Dawn Age," because it was then that the "Age

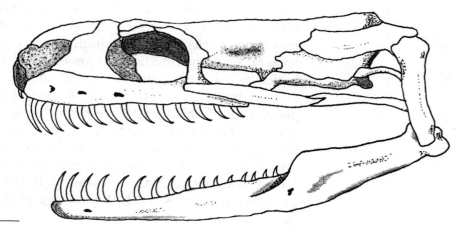

Skull of a python. The teeth are fairly unspecialized, curving to the rear so that they can grasp prey and pull it into the jaws.

of Mammals" truly saw its first light. Mammals, most still small to medium in size, began to spread across the Earth. Birds followed a similar course. And boas, as they still do today, feed almost entirely on mammals and birds. For early boas, the Eocene forests and fields were a cafeteria. So it is no wonder that, along with the creatures upon which they fed, they thrived.

Although primitive in terms of snake genealogy, boids apparently have all the right stuff to survive the vagaries of evolution. Although many are threatened by human activities, such as deforestation and trade in snake hides, they have the basic survival traits to hold their own in nature. One might consider boids as the Model T Fords of snakedom.

Boids kill their prey by constriction; they wrap their muscular bodies around their victim and squeeze. The cause of death is not, as commonly believed, by crushing the body of the prey. Rather, it is by suffocation. As the coils of the snake relentlessly tighten, the lungs of the prey are compressed, so that breathing is restricted and eventually ceases. This method of killing prey seems to have evolved early in the history of snakes. Boids are not the only serpents to kill by constriction. Several other groups of snakes use this method as well, including the North American kingsnake, which feeds mostly on other snakes.

Not as successful as the boids at long-term survival is another group of ancient serpents, which like boas and pythons have vestigial hind legs. The Aniliidae evolved at about the same time as the boidae. Today, however, this group is represented only by one species, a few feet or so long, which spends most of its time burrowing beneath the soils of tropical South America.

The ancestors of modern blindsnakes, which also are burrowers and have degenerate eyes, evolved rather early as well, perhaps in the Paleocene epoch. Most living serpents, however, cannot trace their close lineage nearly that far back. The family of Colubrids, a highly generalized group that composes two-thirds of the snakes now in existence, date to the Oligocene. Among the earliest is a form of water snake, similar to the one that confronted me in my backyard brook. The Elapid family, best known of which are coral snakes and cobras, seem to have waited until the middle of the Miocene period to make their entrance. So did the vipers, candidates for the most advanced snakes by far, and a group which includes rattlesnakes and cottonmouths.

Family Ties

Scientists do not agree on how many families of snakes exist. When it comes to species, there is even more uncertainty. One reason for this is that new species are occasionally discovered. Another is that there are some species of snakes—the kingsnake is a notable example—with myriad subspecies, some so different from one another that they could be developing into entirely new species. By most calculations, the number of living snake species approaches 3,000. A figure often cited is 2700, but it is an estimate.

The following chart is a compilation of snake families drawn from scientific literature. The listing of families and the order in which they appear are not accepted by all taxonomists. Indeed, sometimes it seems that there are as many different methods of classification as there are taxonomists. However, the listing provides a simplified picture of the major groups of snakes in the world, by scientific as well as common name. Another caveat. Many snakes have more than one common name; i.e. "cottonmouth" and "water moccasin." The common names that are given are those that are most often in general useage.

Family Classification of Snakes

1. Anomalepidae (dawn blind snakes)
   Small snakes, some less than a foot long, of South America. They feed on termites.

2. Typhlopidae (blind snakes)
   Mostly tropical, this family of blind snakes is widespread, ranging from South America, through Africa and Asia to Australia. Some species reach temperate regions of southern Asia and Australia.

3. Leptotyphlopidae (threadsnakes *aka* thread blind-snakes)

Small and slender, as befits creatures that slip through the tunnels of termite nests. They are able to actually live within the nests because they secrete a chemical defense against soldier termites. Thus, termites provide these snakes with both room and board, although the snakes are unwelcome guests. Termite nests are built in trees as well as underground, and these snakes have been found in termite cities high in the branches. They inhabit the Americas, tropical Asia and Africa.

4. Acrochordidae (file snakes, wart snakes)

Thick bodied, some species more than six feet long, these are the most aquatic of snakes but for sea snakes; most of them can barely move on land. Their bodies lack the neatly arranged scales of the typical snake and instead have warty scales scattered over loose skin. The name of one of them, the elephant-trunk snake, aptly describes the appearance of this family. These snakes inhabit Southeast Asia and the northern fringes of Australia.

5. Aniliidae (false coral snake)

There is only one species in this family, the last of one of the most ancient lines of snakes. Its common name comes from a red-and-black banding on its body, somewhat similar to the coloration of the venomous coral snake. A yard or so long, it is a burrower that eats small animals, especially other reptiles that live underground. It inhabits South America.

6. Boidae (boas and, depending on the classification system one accepts, pythons)

This group includes the world's largest snakes, the anaconda of South America and the reticulated python of Southeast Asia, which may grow to a length of 30 feet or more. Many other members of the family are almost as large. The boa constrictor can surpass 12 feet in length. Some boas and pythons, however, are much smaller, only a few feet long, even less in the case of boas from the West Indies. It is important to note that some taxonomists view pythons as a separate, but related family to boas. The more traditional view, however, is that boas and pythons constitute a single family. An argument for separating boas from pythons is that the former bear live young while the latter lay eggs. Boas inhabit both the New and Old Worlds. Pythons are strictly an Old World group.

7. Bolyeriidae (Round Island boas)
Up to approximately five feet long, these snakes—two species in all—are very similar to boas. They inhabit the Mascarene Islands in the west Indian Ocean.

8. Loxocemidae (Mexican burrowing python)
Not a true python, this single representative of the family inhabits the Pacific Coast of Mexico and Central America. It lives a partly subterranean life. Secretive and seldom studied by scientists, it eats small mammals, as well as reptiles and reptile eggs.

9. Uropeltidae (pipesnakes and shield-tailed snakes)
Natives of India and Southeast Asia, these snakes spend much of their time below ground. They feed on a variety of small creatures, ranging from lizards to earthworms.

10. Xenopeltidae (sunbeam snake)
Living in the Malay Peninsula and nearby Islands, this snake is the only representative of its family. Like other burrowing snakes with a relatively restricted habitat, its habits are not well known. It lives on small reptiles, mammals, and amphibians.

11. Atractaspididae (African burrowing asps aka mole vipers)
These snakes live underground, where they feed on small, burrowing rodents, especially young in nests. Inhabiting Africa and the west coast of the Arabian Peninsula, they are venomous. Because they operate in very tight quarters, they have a unique method of striking that employs only one of their two venomous fangs, which are located towards the side of the upper jaw, rather in front, in a position similar to the position

of canine teeth in the human jaw. These slip up next to their intended meal, drop their lower jaw so that a fang on the appropriate side is exposed and hook it rearward into their victim.

12. Colubridae (a hodge-podge of snakes)

This family is the boon and bane of taxonomists. From a taxonomist's perspective, it is a catch-all file for "advanced" snakes. It is where species are placed when they cannot be closely related to other, smaller groups. For all practical purposes, this is the family of "typical" snakes. Here are the racers, the rat snakes, the *Natrix* water snakes, the garter snakes, the ringneck snakes—you name it. Most of the serpents that the average American or European encounters belongs to this group. The colubrids include one group of snakes that is venomous. They have large, grooved teeth in the rear of their upper jaw that deliver venom, once the serpent can grab a hold and chew. The venom of many such snakes is mild, designed to stupify or kill small animals. A few of the rear-fanged clan, however, are extremely dangerous to humans. One such is the African boomslang, considered one of the most dan-

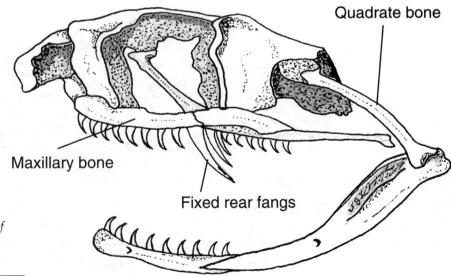

Skull of a boomslang. The enlarged fangs towards the rear of the upper jaw are typical of venomous rear-fanged colubrids.

Quadrate bone

Maxillary bone

Fixed rear fangs

gerous snakes on Earth. The colubrids, if, indeed, they all can be grouped as one family, have the most extensive range of all snake families. They inhabit almost all of the Americas, Africa, and Asia. Only in Australia, which has a corner on animals that are found in few if any other places in the world, are these snakes in the minority. They live only on the northern and western fringes of the island continent.

13. Elapidae (cobras, coral snakes, kraits)
Elapids are snakes of the tropics and subtropics. They are represented in the Americas, including the southern United States, by the coral snakes. Across the bulk of Africa and southern Asia, cobras are the most common elapids. Kraits are another group found in Asia. Australia, which can be considered the cradle of venomous snakes because more than half of the 130 species that live there can deliver a serious jolt of venom, has elapids as well. One of the most feared is the tiger snake, which is noted for its aggressiveness— a trait generally lacking in cobras, despite their nasty reputation. Many elapids, notably the cobras, have inflatable neck hoods. There are also a small number of elapids that are not venomous.

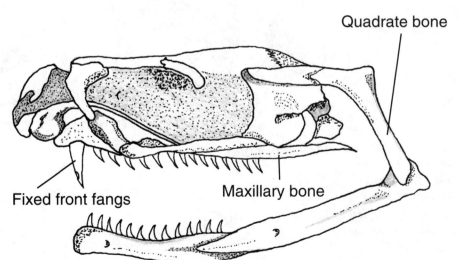

The fangs of venomous elapids, such as this cobra's, are located in the front of the jaw. They are not retractable like those of vipers.

Quadrate bone

Fixed front fangs

Maxillary bone

14. Hydrophidae (sea snakes)

    Sea snakes have an extremely large family of snakes, about 50 species, and widely distributed, virtually throughout the entire tropical portions of the Indo-Pacific ocean. Their bodies are designed for aquatic locomotion. The main body is laterally flattened; the tail is horizontally compressed, like an oar or rudder. The body, like that of an eel, helps the snake slip through the resistance of water with little effort. The tail, used for steering and propulsion, probably functions both for locomotive power and steering. Scientists usually divide the sea snakes into two sub-families; the Laticudines, which lay eggs on shore, and the Hydrophiines, which bear live young in the water. These snakes are the true sea serpents, living their entire lives in the ocean. Even types that lay eggs ashore can barely move on land. They are not aggressive but are among the most venomous of snakes.

15. Viperidae (vipers and pit vipers)

    With their triangular heads, long and erectile fangs, and stout bodies, these are the average person's image of a venomous snake. No wonder. They have the

Viper skull. This diagram depicts the resting position of viper fangs and how they erect when the snake is striking. Note the interior venom tube in the fang.

Quadrate bone

Maxillary bone

Retractable fangs

widest range of any snake family, except for the colubrids. They are found throughout Africa, the southern half of North America, all of South America except for the eastern fringe of the continent, and Eurasia up to the fringes of the Arctic. They are absent from Australia, probably because that continent sailed away from the rest of the Earth's land masses before this

COAT OF MANY COLORS

By their genes you will know them. That, basically, is one way in which scientists can now describe what constitutes a species. The basic gene pattern of all individuals in a species is the same, written in stone. Beyond that, members of a species can readily interbreed to produce fertile young. Mules are not capable of reproducing their own kind because they are hybrids of horse and donkey, both in the same genus, but of different species. Homo sapiens—that's us—is a species. We may vary in details such as skin color, typical body size, and facial details. But inside, we are all the same—and when we mate, we reproduce other individuals of our species.

The common kingsnake is a species, Lampropeltis getulus. Common kingsnakes live mostly across the lower half of the United States and into Mexico. Their northern limits are coastal Oregon and New Jersey. Within this vast area, common kingsnakes display a remarkable array of different color patterns. Many factors, including geographic isolation and adaptation to local conditions, play a role in the differences. The varieties of the common kingsnake are considered subspecies. Seven subspecies of common kingsnake are recognized. To the uninitiated eye, they might seem to be entirely different species of snakes. For example, the eastern kingsnake (L.g. getulus), which ranges from southern New Jersey to Florida, and west to the Appalachians, is chocolate-brown with whitish crossbands that resemble links of a chain. Its two colors contrast markedly, making it very conspicuous. Other kingsnakes, to varying degrees, have markings that lack such contrast. The Florida kingsnake (L.g. floridiana), with scattered populations in northeastern Florida, can be brown or olive and while it, too, has light chain-like markings, they often are barely visible. The speckled kingsnake (L.g. holbrooki) of the Midwest, eastern Texas, Mississippi and Alabama, has scales that range from dark brown to black. There are only remnants of crossbands on its body, which instead is covered with white or yellow speckles that give it a salt-and-pepper appearance. Crossbands and spots are found in the other subspecies of common kingsnakes, as well, and these also vary widely in their boldness of color. The California kingsnake (L.g. californiae) is dark brown to black with crossbands or a dark stripe. The black kingsnake (L.g. Niger) is black, with chains of small light speckles. These snakes can interbreed, which causes even more variations in color.

family appeared. The trademark of this family is a pair of fangs that lie back in the upper jaw when not in use but, hinged by specialized bones, snap out into an erect position for striking. The distinction between vipers, such as the heavy Gabon viper of Africa, and the pit vipers, rattlesnakes and copperheads, has to do with heat-sensing organs. The pit vipers have pitted organs, one on each side of the head, that enable them to sense heat produced by the bodies of warm-blooded prey. They are, in effect, heat-seeking missiles—perhaps more up to date in that respect than any other predators, in terms of biotechnology.

A

B

Some varieties of the common kingsnake:

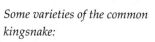

A. eastern kingsnake (lampropeltis getulus getula)

B. striped California kingsnake hatchling (lampropeltis getulus californiae)

C. black kingsnake (lampropeltis getulus nigrita)

C

WIL MARA

Legless Wonders

Snakes share myriad features with other reptiles but, obviously, also have characteristics that are unique. Combined, these traits describe a snake.

The Skins Game

The outer layer of a snake's skin is covered by scales, similar to those on lizards. Scales are hard and made of a material similar to the keratin in human fingernails and hair. (Crocodilians and turtles have scales as well, but theirs are fortified with bone, and called "scutes.") Contrary to a popular belief that snakes are slimy, they are indeed smooth characters. Their scales—which can number in the thousands—form a smooth and, hard as they are, flexible protection over the snake's body. Scales are an armor of sorts. They help protect the snake against enemies, although they do not offer the solid protection of scutes. They do quite well, however, shielding the snake against the extremes of heat and cold and also help seal moisture into the body, a major plus in hot, dry areas where many snakes live.

A few species of snakes groom their scales by polishing them with a secretion of a viscous fluid that emanates from an opening near the nose. The merit of polishing is uncertain, but it seems to keep the scales in good condition, as people who put mink oil on their boots and polish on their shoes have discovered.

Even if polished, a snake's scaly skin gradually wears out, just like a pair of old shoes. Scales wear away and must be replaced. And just as growing children need larger shoes and

Boomslang scale patterns. Not all snake scales are the same. Various species have scales in different arrangements and configuration. Some vipers, for example, have rough, horny scales. Colubrids, like this boomslang, have flattened scales. The size and shape of its scales differ according to their location on the body.

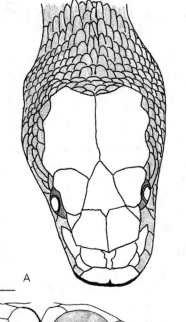

A

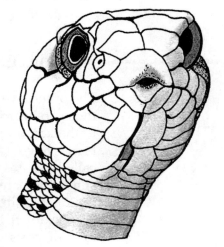

B

C

24

An individual snake's scales vary in shape and size according to where they are on the body. The scales under the lower jaw of this black racer are much more elongated than those on the rest of its body.

LINDA KRULIKOWSKI

A close-up look at the scales of a northern pine snake (red variety).

WIL MARA

WIL MARA

The opaque eyes of this eastern hognose snake indicate that it is ready to shed.

clothing, a growing snake—and snakes grow throughout their lives—needs a new skin. So, periodically, snakes shed their skin, as do lizards. The shedding of skin in snakes and lizards adds to evidence that birds evolved from reptiles. Birds molt old feathers—feathers are modified scales—and grow fresh ones, just as snakes trade old scales for new.

The intervals between sheddings vary, ranging from several weeks to months. Scientists believe that factors such as temperature of the surroundings and diet, which influence growth, determine when it is time for a snake to have a new skin. It is easy to figure out when a snake is preparing to shed by looking at its eyes. The eyes of a snake become cloudy with a buildup of fluid that enables a snake to slough off the clear outer scale covering each eye, to be replaced by new ones. Experienced snake handlers know that this is the time to treat serpents gingerly. Blinded, they react aggressively to intrusion.

When a snake sheds, it literally crawls out of its own skin. The process begins at the snake's lips, where the skin begins to break, usually when the snake rubs it against objects such as rocks, twigs, or whatever else in its vicinity happens to be solid.

The snake's own bodily movements also help crack and remove its skin. Snakes that are beginning to shed their skin yawn repeatedly to break open the skin around the mouth.

Once the envelope of skin is opened at the mouth, the snake rubs its body on the ground, against branches of whatever else it can find to help it undress. There is considerable evidence that the snake also uses muscular contractions to divest itself of its old garb. The shed skin is literally turned inside out. If you have ever removed a jacket or bathrobe in a hurry and left the sleeves inverted, you can understand the process. As the snake moves forward, the old skin peels off backwards so that the position of the tail and the head of the shed skin are reversed from what they were when on the snake. The entire operation may take only minutes for some snakes and seldom more than a half-hour in most. After all is finished, the snake has a new set of clothes, shiny, smooth and unworn.

Getting Around Without Legs

Humans, especially when they age, have problems with their backbone, the column of little bones called "vertebrae," that is the support of the spinal column and anchor of the skeleton. We strive for flexible backbones, with exercise and expensive beds. A stiff backbone creates a stiff and, often, painful back. Humans have 33 vertebrae in their backbone. Snakes have up to 300 or so, each attached to a rib on either side. Given all those vertebrae, one might think that snakes are highly susceptible to back problems. However, the backbone of a snake is innately flexible and the key to its means of locomotion. Unlike animals that stand on legs, a snake does not need a particularly rigid backbone to support its body. Rather, it relies on a backbone that—apologies to Chubby Checker—does the twist, and several other kinds of sinuous moves.

Snakes have four different modes of locomotion, not all of which are used by every species. All but one of their methods are variations of the twist. Each method depends on the traction of board scales on the snake's belly. These scales, linked by muscles to the ribs, grip the substrate, whether it is the ground or a

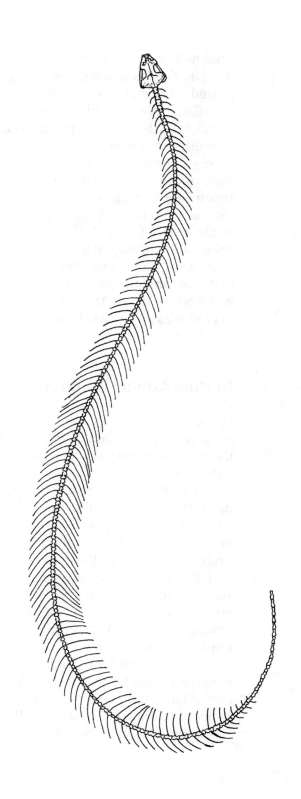

A snake's skeleton. The flexible backbone allows for the snake's undulating means of locomotion.

branch, as the muscles contract and relax, propelling the snake in the direction it chooses to go.

The basic means of serpentine locomotion is what scientists term "lateral undulation." Boiled down to layman's language, this type of travel is relatively simple. The snake curves portions of its body to the side, in the shape of an **S**. As it does so, the snake uses whatever is beneath to push itself forward. It is an extremely efficient use of force. As martial artists will note, pressure full-force ahead takes far more energy than using

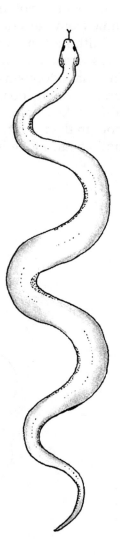

Lateral undulation

leverage to the side, especially if the leverage is gained by the long body of a snake.

Another movement is called the "concertina," after a musical instrument that was the predecessor of the accordion. (This method of locomotion is also called the "accordion movement." The snake's body works similarly to the bellows of a concertina or, if you would have it, an accordion. In effect, the body lengthens and contracts like a bellows to move the snake along. The forward part of its body reaches out and gains traction; then the rest of the body is hauled in the direction of movement. Another method, used by desert snakes, gains its name from the sidewinder rattlesnake of western North America, although many other types of serpents use it. It is a sideways version of lateral movement, using the typical **S** motion. The snake loops its body to the side, creating a trough in the sand or other loose earth. Once the initial move is made, the tail, hooked into the trough, provides leverage for another loop. In the right type of soil, a snake that uses this sort of locomotion can move incredibly fast and quite deceptively, which

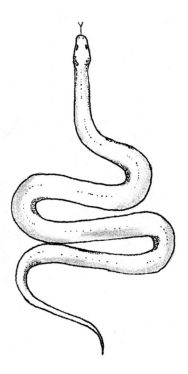

Concertina movement

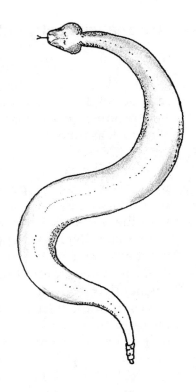

Sidewinder movement

is why sneak thieves and backshooters of the Old West were sometimes called "sidewinders."

Along with all their fancy moves, sometimes snakes just push ahead. This is a good way to move over smooth ground or in a tight space. The snake uses its belly scales like treads on a bulldozer. From front to rear, the scales contact the ground with a ripple effect and the attached muscles pull the snake forward, rather like the movement of an earthworm.

Forward movement (like earthworm or caterpillar)

Are Snakes Really Cold-Blooded?

Technically, snakes are not cold blooded. That outmoded term was used to describe the fact that modern reptiles and amphibians do not have the capacity to use food as a source of bodily heat production, as birds and mammals can. Some ancient reptiles such as dinosaurs, probably ancestors of birds, and therapsids, whose line led to mammals, may have had that capability. Be that as it may, no matter how much they eat, snakes can regulate their body temperature only by adjusting to their surroundings. The ideal body temperature for your average snake is in the mid-eighties F., although it can survive under conditions many degrees higher and several lower. If the environment around a snake is too hot, it must seek a cool spot, like a cave, an underground burrow or, simply, shade. Desert snakes frequently creep into the burrows of rodents to shield themselves from the heat of the sun, and they may obtain a meal at the same time. If a snake chills, it must position itself in a situation where it can soak up heat. Water snakes needing a warm-up bask on logs, as do turtles. Snakes that are adapted to an arboreal life may climb to the treetops to get a bit of sun. The instinct of a snake to find warmth when it is cold works well in

A copperhead basks in the sun. By extending its body, it can soak up more of the sun's heat.

LINDA KRULIKOWSKI

32

nature, but in a world dominated by humans, it can be counter-productive. Why are so many snakes killed on roads? Because the road surface retains heat, even after the sun goes down. During the cool of night, or on chilly days, snakes are drawn to roadways, where they try to warm themselves, stretched out and vulnerable to traffic. The result is often a squashed snake, sometimes by accident, other times by drivers who—given the antipathy of many people towards snakes—deliberately run over them.

In areas of the world with cold winters, snakes become dormant. They look for sheltered spots, like caves and crevices, where they can shelter themselves from the cold. Their bodily functions are depressed so that their metabolism operates at an extremely low level, in a reptilian version of mammalian hibernation. Typically, snakes inhabiting cold climates spend the winter underground, below the frost line, so that cells in their bodies do not freeze. Given their low level of metabolism at this time, they do not need food. When dormant, snakes can tolerate cold that would kill them if they were active; it appears that various chemicals in the snake's body may serve as a form of natural antifreeze. Many species of snakes hibernate communally in dens, and sometimes these sanctuaries contain more than one species. Timber rattlesnakes and copperheads, for instance, often share dens.

Reproduction

As noted in the previous chapter, reptiles evolved from the amphibians, which, in turn, arose from fishes. Amphibians were the first vertebrates with the ability to live on land. However, they never completely severed their links with water, in which many of them spend the majority of their time. Amphibians need moisture to prevent desiccation of their bodies. Their skin must be moist in order for them to breed. Importantly, their eggs, lacking shells, must stay moist in order to survive. Unlike amphibians, but like birds, reptiles produce eggs with shells which are usually leathery, not smooth and hard like those of birds. The shelled egg was a signal advance in the evolution of vertebrates. The shell encloses fluids, which keeps the embry-

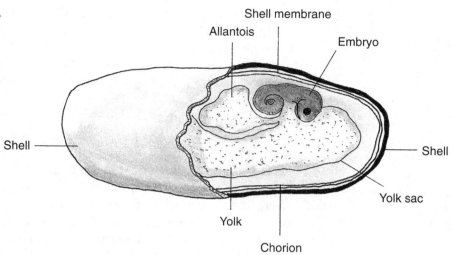

Diagram of a snake egg. The snake egg is very similar to the egg of a bird. The egg is encased in a shell, lined by a shell membrane and another membrane called the chorion. The allantois is yet another membrane that grows and surrounds the embryo, protecting it. The embryo is linked to a sac containing nourishing yolk. Unlike snakes that bear living young, those that hatch from shelled eggs have an "egg tooth," which helps them crack through the shell.

onic reptile moist, freeing reptile reproduction from dependence on water. It enabled reptiles to reproduce on land—even aquatic reptiles, such as sea turtles and sea snakes—come ashore to lay their eggs. With the ability to reproduce their kind on land, reptiles were able to spread over a far greater range of habitats than amphibians, enhancing their immense diversity.

The snake egg is similar to a bird's egg. The embryonic snake is shielded, from the outside in, by a shell and membranes, some of which are formed when the egg is within the female, others after it is laid. Like embryonic birds, snakes in the egg are nourished by yolk, a present from the mother.

Absolutes seldom hold true in nature. Some reptiles, including snakes such as boas, do not lay eggs but, instead, bear living young. Can these reptiles be considered viviparous, a term often applied to them? Technically, no. Their embryos live in eggs that are retained within the mother's body, independent of the fluidic life support that embryonic mammals receive. The appropriate term for such snakes is "ovoviviparous."

Most female snakes have two ovaries, elongated and partially overlapping, one slightly ahead of the other. Eggs arise in the ovaries and then move to the oviduct. The eggs are fertilized in the ovaries by sperm from the male, delivered by means of a two-pronged copulatory organ, the hemipenes. Fertilization is accomplished via the cloaca, a vent in the body—which reptiles

LINDA KRULIKOWSKI

A new-born copperhead emerges from its birth sac.

have in common with birds and amphibians—where excretory and reproductive systems open. The females of some snakes are able to store sperm in the oviduct for months after mating. Many North American rattlesnakes mate as summer draws to a close, but the female does not produce mature eggs, ready to be

LINDA KRULIKOWSKI

After emerging from their sacs, young copperheads remain in the vicinity of the mother for a short time, then depart. This youngster crawls over its mother's body prior to leaving her.

fertilized, until the following spring. The females of species whose young hatch externally from eggs—most snakes—have a gland that produces the shell in the ovaries.

Snake courtship can be an elaborate affair. The male often chases the female, rubbing against her and flicking his tongue onto her body. The male's efforts are designed to allow the pair to intertwine, so that their cloacas can meet, at which point the male inserts his hemipenis. Sea snakes, taking a cue from fish, often mate in swarms, with males jostling for position so that they can join with females. Often, successful mating results from who gets there first with the most. Many male terrestrial snakes must address the question of rivals before mating. Many, such as rattlesnakes and mambas, engage in what animal behaviorists call "combat dances," in order to gain rights to a female. These are ritualized battles—rattlesnakes generally do not bite one another—but are very much a test of muscle and might. The two males posture and pose, rising and writhing, like professional grapplers at the beginning of a match; but then they really do wrestle, entwining their bodies, each snake trying to

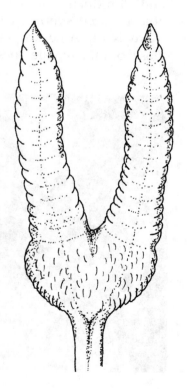

Hemipenes of a rattlesnake. Male snakes have a paired sexual organ that fits into corresponding openings in the female. Coincidentally, sharks have a similar arrangement.

WIL MARA

Florida scarlet snakes joined in mating.

bring the other low by pinning it to the ground. Other snakes simply go at it without the preliminary posturing. Competing male anacondas engage in violent mat work, struggling on the ground. Imagine two bodies, perhaps 15 to 20-plus feet long, almost as much as a utility pole and virtually all muscle, strug-

Ritualized battle of male western diamondbacks. These combats seldom inflict injury. There is a lot of posturing, and some pushing and shoving, but they are seldom if ever fights to the death.

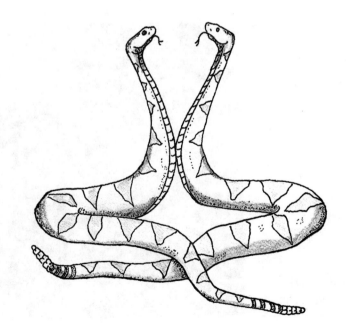

gling for supremacy on the rain forest floor. The struggle seems to be quite violent, but usually combats between male snakes over females are not designed to result in death. The loser, once overwhelmed, generally departs posthaste. The winner generally lets him go. After all, why expend any more energy on fighting when it is needed for procreation?

Prolific Mammas

Female snakes look for hidden spots to produce their young, such as crevices, the interior of fallen logs, tunnels, and caves. Young of species that are born alive, rather than hatch from eggs, arrive in the world encapsulated in a clear membrane, which they rapidly rupture. Hatchlings of snakes that emerge from shelled egg break through the shell of the egg by slitting it with a small, sharp projection on the end of their snouts, called the "egg tooth." This structure is also found in hatchling birds. It may take a day, or even a few days, before the young snake finally leaves the egg.

A northern pine snake hatching from its egg.

WIL MARA

LINDA KRULIKOWSKI

The vivid markings of this newly-born northern water snake will fade with age as the snake skin becomes darker.

Snakes can produce a prodigious amount of young. Garter snakes have been known to have more than 70 young, although the average number is much lower. Some pythons can have over 100 progeny. Rattlesnakes can have a couple of dozen. Since parental care of young is non-existent, except in a few species of egg-laying snakes, mass production of new generations helps species survival.

CARE GIVERS

Pythons are very good mothers, in serpentine terms. They coil around their eggs, shielding them from enemies and the elements. There is fairly solid scientific evidence that the mother python goes a step further than pure protection. Reptiles do not generate body heat, as mammals and birds do. However, the females of some pythons seem able to give off slight amounts of warmth while brooding their eggs, apparently by contractions of their muscles.

Some female cobras, especially the king cobra, actively guard their eggs. The king cobra, unlike other snakes, builds a nest of vegetation in which her eggs are deposited. Although the king cobra is rather docile, stories about this species chasing humans may stem from incidents in which females have mounted a defense of the nest. The vegetation provides shelter for the eggs and, as it rots, the heat of decomposition helps incubate the embryos.

Jaws

Snakes are famed for engulfing mammoth meals. "Engulfing" is an appropriate term, as the snake swallows its food whole, by grasping it in its mouth and then, literally, by crawling over it. The snake holds the prey in its jaws, working it down by moving its jaws and head to and fro, while it pushes its body forward. Once the meal enters the body, the snake's ribs expand, an easy task because while they are connected to the backbone, there is no breastbone link in front. The elastic skin of the snake can accommodate the bulk of a large victim. Until a meal is digested, which may take from hours to days, it is evident as a large bulge within the snake's body.

A snake can ingest a victim several times the diameter of its head or body. A garter snake, a half-inch or so across, can swallow a toad, with a body bulkier than a golf ball, not to mention its long hind legs. A large anaconda or python, with a body diameter of, perhaps, a foot, can easily take down a deer or pig that weighs 50 pounds, and often animals that are even larger. The secret of the snake's ability to swallow large prey, aside from its skeletal flexibility, lies in its lower jaw. The bones of the left and right sides of the jaw do not meet at the front. Instead, they are hinged by stretchy ligaments, allowing each side of the jaw to move independently; the lower jaw bones are also jointed in the middle. The lower jawbones are loosely attached at the rear to the quadrate bones, which in lizards are fixed to the skull but in snakes are moveable. This entire arrangement provides the jaws of a snake with an enormous gape and the ability to maneuver around prey of different sizes and shapes.

EGG ON ITS FACE

Ironically, a certain snake, about a yard long and not much more than a couple of inches in circumference can demonstrate the ability of small serpents to ingest relatively huge items of food as well as do the huge pythons and anacondas. The egg-eating snake of Africa feeds solely on what its name implies, the eggs of birds, some of which are as large as Grade A chicken eggs.

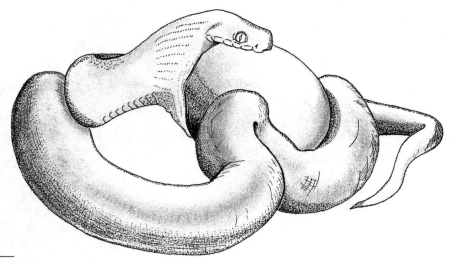

Egg-eating snakes have carried the ability of snakes to widen the gap of their jaws and swallow proportionately large prey to the maximum.

This snake has unique adaptations to its unique diet. It possesses an immense gape for its size. As the egg is being swallowed down the snake's throat, its way smoothed by glandular fluids, it comes into contact with pointed projections on the upper vertebrae, which puncture and crush the shell. The contents of the egg are ingested and the shell fragments ejected from the snake's mouth.

Inner Workings

Overall, the inner organs that enable a snake to metabolize food, to eliminate waste and to breathe, work in similar fashion to those of other reptiles, and even to those of birds and mammals. However, since it does not chew its food, the snake has extremely powerful digestive enzymes. Snakes rid themselves of waste in the form of feces and urine, as do other vertebrates. However, the urine of snakes, and most other reptiles, is not liquid; it is solid or partially solid, helping the snake's body conserve water. This is especially important for snakes inhabiting dry areas.

The circulatory system of snakes and lizards is not unlike that of birds and mammals, but there still are differences. The

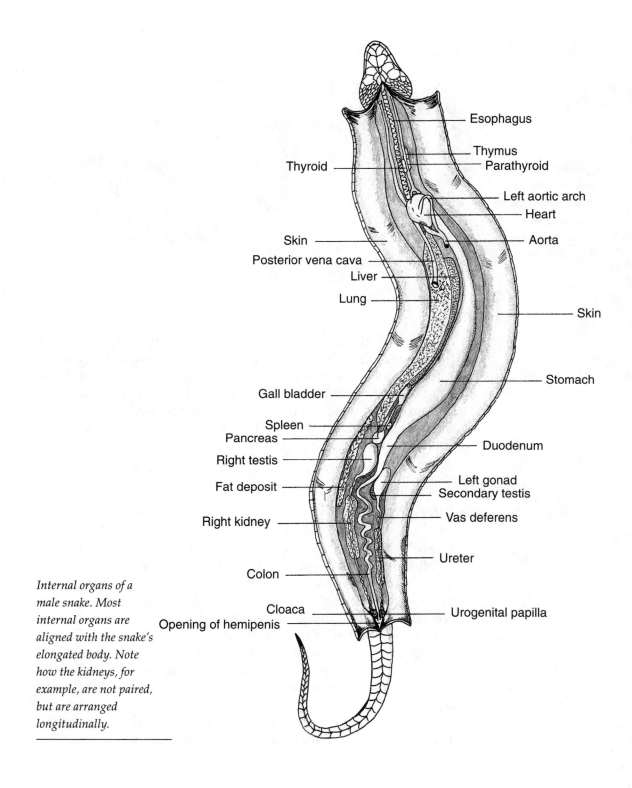

Esophagus

Thymus
Parathyroid

Thyroid

Left aortic arch
Heart

Skin

Aorta

Posterior vena cava

Liver

Lung

Skin

Stomach

Gall bladder

Spleen
Pancreas

Duodenum

Right testis

Fat deposit

Left gonad
Secondary testis

Right kidney

Vas deferens

Ureter

Colon

Cloaca

Opening of hemipenis

Urogenital papilla

Internal organs of a male snake. Most internal organs are aligned with the snake's elongated body. Note how the kidneys, for example, are not paired, but are arranged longitudinally.

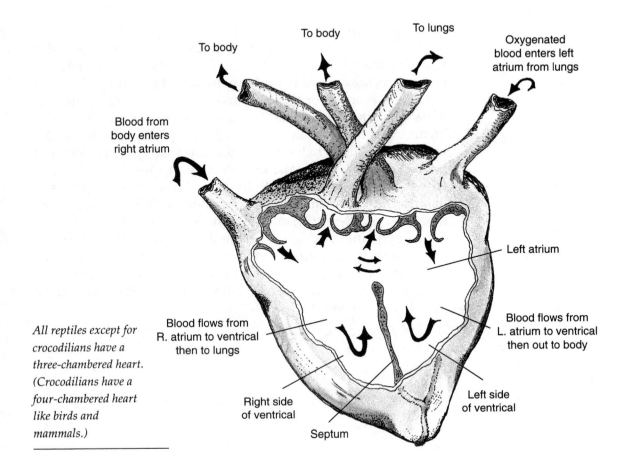

To body

To body

To lungs

Oxygenated
blood enters left
atrium from lungs

Blood from
body enters
right atrium

Left atrium

*All reptiles except for
crocodilians have a
three-chambered heart.
(Crocodilians have a
four-chambered heart
like birds and
mammals.)*

Blood flows from
R. atrium to ventrical
then to lungs

Blood flows from
L. atrium to ventrical
then out to body

Right side
of ventrical

Left side
of ventrical

Septum

key difference is that the snake has only one ventricle in its heart, with two halves. The two chambers of the heart ventricle in birds and mammals (as well as crocodilians) are separated by a membrane, making them distinct chambers. This gives the snake a three-chambered, rather than a four-chambered, heart. (The other two chambers in all of these creatures are the right and left atrium.)

Blood from which oxygen has been used up enters the left atrium of the snake's heart, passes into the right half of the ventricle and then via arteries to the lungs, where it picks up another cargo of oxygen. From there, the blood travels through veins to the heart's left atrium, then into the left half of the ventricle and, after that through arteries to the body, which metabolizes the oxygen. A small amount of oxygenated and deoxygenated blood mixes in the snake's single ventricle, causing the lungs to work harder. This process is not quite as efficient as in creatures with a four-chambered heart; that setup prevents contact between blood carrying oxygen to the body from that returning and seeking another pickup of this gaseous element, enabling animals to metabolize their food. Snakes take in oxygen just as we do, by breathing it from air. Even sea snakes, superbly adapted to the water, must, like whales, rise to the surface to breathe. When it inhales oxygen, the snake exhales carbon dioxide, a gas that, when it builds up, is toxic to humans, but is used by plants to manufacture food through photosynthesis. In that respect, the snake is no different than a human. Animals use oxygen, produced by plants during photosynthesis, to live. Plants use carbon dioxide to live and eliminate oxygen as waste. The exquisite trade-off keeps life alive on our planet and is an infinitely complex, yet simple, bio-engineered system of give-and-take, a grand design, if you will.

What Makes Snakes Tick

Although all snakes share basic behavioral patterns, such as seeking out surroundings that will either warm them up or cool them down, there is a wide variation of behaviors among different species. As in other animals, behavior is influenced largely by the senses, which react to stimuli, or cues, from the outside; the eye reacting to movement is an example. It could be said that snakes have the same five senses as most other vertebrates: sight, smell, hearing, taste, and touch. However, some of these senses operate minimally or are combined, while others—at least, in the case of some snakes—are super keen, functioning on a level far above those of humans. The snake's sense of touch, for instance, is similar to ours. However, due to the serpent's coating of scales, it may not be as sensitive, except, perhaps, in the area of the snout, the business end of the snake when it comes to finding and eating food. Since snakes lack an eardrum, they do not hear in the way that we do, but their ability to sense vibrations does alert them to movement in their vicinity.

Vision

As with most vertebrates, snakes rely to a significant degree on vision to gather sensory information. The basic pattern of a snake's eye structure is similar to that of other reptiles, as well as that of birds and mammals, but with some differences. The amount of light entering the lens of the vertebrate eye is controlled by the iris, which expands in low-light situations and contracts in bright illumination. When the light falls on the retina, behind the eyeball an image is registered and sent to the brain via the optic nerve. The lens is flexible, allowing for adjustment to distance. In the human eye, and that of lizards, the lens flattens when long-distance viewing is needed and bulges when a close-up view is mandated. The snake's lens works in a different way. Instead of changing shape, it moves back and forth; forward to see near objects, backwards to view those at a distance. No other vertebrate, indeed, no other animal has this arrangement. Scientists believe that most, if not all, snakes do not see color. If true, it is not a handicap, because snakes have many other sensory mechanisms that help them discern their environment. One of these is the tongue.

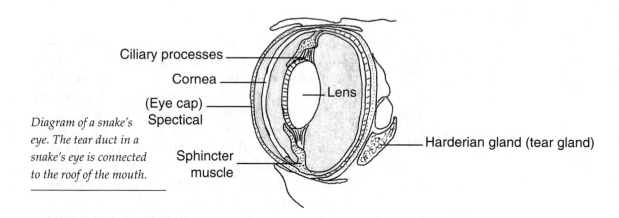

Diagram of a snake's eye. The tear duct in a snake's eye is connected to the roof of the mouth.

Ciliary processes

Cornea

(Eye cap) Spectical

Lens

Sphincter muscle

Harderian gland (tear gland)

BLIND AS A SNAKE

The so-called "blindsnakes," a primitive family widespread in the tropics and subtropics almost world-wide, are barely able to see. Each of their eyes is covered by a cloudy scale. Blindsnakes cannot perceive images, only changes in light. However, sight is not a particularly useful sense for these snakes. They live mainly underground where they feed mainly on termites and ants.

A Forked Tongue

Among the most misunderstood organs of the snake is its forked tongue. For example, there is the old saw, "He speaks with forked tongue." It has been attributed to Native Americans but it probably was the invention of a writer of Western lore because many tribes, such as the Hopi and Cherokee, revere snakes. And it very likely evolved from Judeo-Christian antipathy towards snakes. After all, the serpent lied to Eve. Many Biblical images of the temptation of Eve show the satanic serpent, coiled near the original First Lady, with its lascivious tongue flicking out in her direction, inviting her to eat that Big Apple. She did, and it was a bad move on her part.

Another myth about the snake's tongue is that it is a "stinger." Wrong. The tongue of a snake is no more a weapon than a human's and is much more delicate. It is a highly sensitive organ that, unlike the human tongue, is not so much one of tasting and helping ingest food, but an aid in finding it.

The human tongue is covered with the openings of taste buds, which underneath the skin open into nerve endings that transmit messages to the brain. (Even so, as wine tasters know, the center of human taste bud activity lies in the palate.) Snakes also have taste buds, although most do not

A copperhead extends its tongue to test the environment for chemical signals.

LINDA KRULIKOWSKI

possess them in abundance. There is some evidence that some snakes can taste the difference between something good to eat and something noxious—so they can reject a foul meal. Nevertheless, the sense of taste, in its purest form, is not a primary sense of snakes.

However, in snakes, as well as all vertebrates, the senses of taste and smell are related. Both depend upon sensing chemicals in the environment rather than upon mechanical cues, such as movement, which trigger visual messages to the brain. The snake's tongue helps the snake sense odors in its surroundings. Although the tongue of a snake cannot smell, it is a transfer mechanism to an organ that can. This is the Jacobson's organ, two cavities located above the roof of the mouth, walled with cells sensitive to chemical odors. Each cavity has its own small opening through the snake's palate. It was named for the researcher who discovered it, L. L. Jacobson, a Dane. And, now, the secret of why a snake has a forked tongue, and why it constantly flicks out of the organ. The tongue picks up scented molecules, mostly from surfaces such as the ground, that are around the snake. Each of the two forks is inserted into one of the Jacobson's organ openings. The organ analyses the scents and relays its information to the brain. Data received by the brain helps the snake identify all sorts of things, from the trail left by prey to that of a potential mate. Since the Jacobson's organ depends on molecules gathered by the tongue, it is primarily a short-range sensor. After all, although it may look long, the tongue of a snake is only inches in length; it seems longer because the snake can extend most of its length from the sheath in which it lies. For

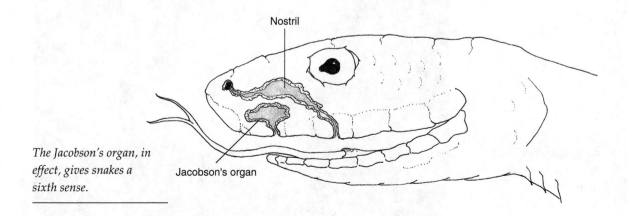

Nostril

Jacobson's organ

The Jacobson's organ, in effect, gives snakes a sixth sense.

Eastern coral snake (Micurus fulvius)

A copperhead (Agkistrodon contortrix) displaying erect fangs.

Two copperheads on a ledge near their den

Eastern diamondback rattlesnake (Crotalus adamanteus)

An aroused timber rattlesnake raises its rattle.

Sidewinder (Crotalus cerastes)

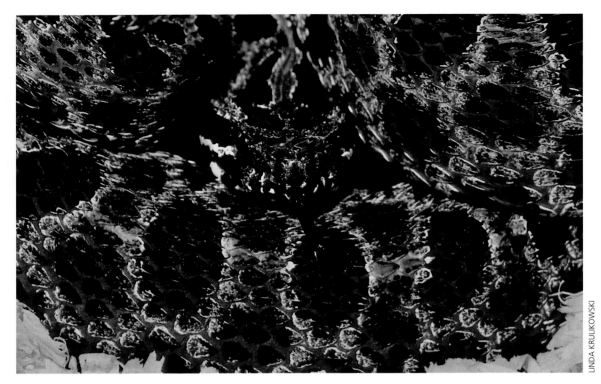

Dusky pygmy rattlesnake (Sistrurus milarius barbouri)

Carolina pigmy rattlesnake (red variety: Sistrurus milarius milarius)

Namibian spitting cobra (Naja nigricollis nigricollitis)

Rhinoceros viper (Bitis nasicornis)

Banded krait (Bungarus caeruleus)

Asiatic cobra (Naja naja)

King cobra (Ophiophagus hannah)

A close-up view of the head of the Malaysian long-glanded coral snake (Manticora bivirgata flaviceps)

McMahon's viper (Eristocophis macmahoni)

Pope's tree viper (Trimeresurus popeorum)

long-range smell, the snake relies on its nose. The nose receives scents from the air, which means that it can work at longer range than the Jacobson's organ, and get a whiff, for example, of a mouse a substantial distance away.

Hot on the Trail

Along with smells taken in by nose and particles carried to the Jacobson's organ by the tongue, certain snakes, notably the rattlesnakes and other pit vipers, but also, to a lesser degree, some boas and pythons, have organs on their faces that enable them to track "warm-blooded" prey (mammals and birds) by the body heat that these creatures produce. This is why that pit vipers have been called "heat-seeking missiles." They literally "see" in the infrared portion of the spectrum. Long before the military and law enforcement establishments were using infrared optics to find objects in the darkness of night, rattlesnakes were doing what comes naturally.

The beautiful biofeedback of evolution has dictated that rattlesnakes hunt warm-blooded prey by night, when the menu for dinner, featuring rodents such as mice and rats, is also

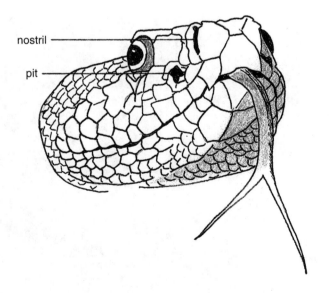

nostril

pit

Head of a pit viper showing placement of nostril and pit.

active. Rattlesnakes are among the most proficient of nature's night stalkers because their ability to image prey by its body heat gives them an immense edge.

Heat is carried by waves of energy, just as are light and sound. Waves of energy move through media, whether it is the void of space, air, water or, especially in the case of earthquakes, solid ground. The human eye can perceive certain forms of light energy within the Newtonian spectrum. It cannot see ultraviolet, at the upper end of the spectrum, nor can it see infrared, at the lower. The rattlesnake can "see" images in infrared, even if it may not be able to discern them in detail.

The rattlesnake sees in infrared by using cells that are similar to those that sense warmth in the human skin. In humans, these cells are scattered, only a couple per square inch of skin. The rattlesnake, on the other hand, has hundreds of thousands of these cells jammed into the two pits located below the eyes on its snout, several times more than on the entire human body.

Pit vipers such as the rattlesnake may be the most finely tuned predators on Earth. An experiment by scientist T. H. Bullock at the University of California lends credence to this point. In 1952, Bullock decided to check out the senses by which a rattlesnake finds its prey. His experiment was ingenious and helped pinpoint the role of the pits that lend their name to the

The heat-sensing pits are clearly visible on the snout of this timber rattlesnake.

LINDA KRULIKOWSKI

pit vipers. He covered the eyes of a rattler with adhesive tape; no easy job. Then he chemically blocked the olfactory senses by spraying a sedative into its mouth. He placed the rattlesnake in a small cage and dropped in a mouse, a tasty tidbit for a rattler. Blinded and deprived of smell, the rattlesnake had no trouble hunting. As the mouse scurried about in alarm, the snake intently tracked it. The snake went into its typical striking posture, a coil and then its head shot out, its fangs striking the mouse dead. After a few minutes, the mouse had disappeared down the snake's gullet.

Unable to see or smell, and with hearing not a real factor in the snake's ability to perceive, the rattler nevertheless targeted and nailed its prey. Bullock was curious. He examined the snake and probed the two small pits that he noticed on each side of the snake's snout. He repeated his test, blocking the olfactory sense and the eyes—and, this time, taping the pits shut. He placed what amounted to a herd of mice in the cage. A day went by, then a few more. Not one of the mice had been captured by the snake.

Bullock examined the pits and found the masses of heat-sensitive nerve cells. Subsequent research determined that, using these cells, a rattlesnake can distinguish the difference of a fraction of a degree in temperature difference between an object—a mouse, for example—and its surroundings. This helps it pinpoint prey. This heat sense is not infallible, however. A light bulb, turned off but still warm, was wrapped in cloth and, in darkness, introduced to a rattlesnake. The snake struck the bulb.

The Prey

The food-gathering mechanics of a snake are geared towards one goal—eating other animals. There are few, if any, absolutes in science, but one may be that there never has been a snake that eats plants.

Animals eaten by snakes include snails, slugs, earthworms, amphibians, insects, lizards, birds, mammals—and other snakes. The king cobra is a notorious snake eater. In fact, snakes are its main prey. King cobras are not very discriminating when it comes to the types of snakes that they will consume. Just about any snake they can overcome and swallow fits the bill. "Junior," a huge king cobra that lived at the Bronx Zoo for many years, had a penchant for feeding on his mates and ate several of them.

Most snakes have a preferred list of prey, although even within a single species it may vary according to the habitat in which the snake lives. Garter snakes living in dry areas tend to eat small terrestrial invertebrates, while those in places where ponds and streams are abundant seek out fish and frogs. The indigo snake, found in Georgia and Florida and from Texas to South America, is a true generalist as far as diet is concerned. Frogs, lizards, other snakes, turtles, small mammals, and birds are on its menu. Most rattlesnakes live mainly on small mammals, especially rodents, but they will consume birds—especially the nestlings of ground birds—if the chance arises.

A goodly number of snakes are true gourmets, with a tightly restricted diet. The cat-eyed snake of the American tropics sups mainly on the eggs of certain tree frogs. It finds its meals in trees, not in the water. Some species of tropical tree frogs lay their eggs on leaves, above temporary pools that form in the rainy season. When the tadpoles hatch, they fall into the water and continue their development if not eaten by this predator. Several types of snakes found in various parts of the globe feed

This young mangrove salt marsh snake (Nerodia clarki compressicauda) is well-adapted to eating fish.

WIL MARA

WIL MARA

As its name suggests, the Graham's crayfish snake (Regina grahami) specializes in eating crayfish.

almost exclusively on slugs and snails. Slugs, with their soft, exposed bodies, present no problem, but the shells of snails are a defense that must be surmounted. Some of these "slug-eating" snakes have hooked teeth that extract the snail's body from its shell in the manner of an escargot fork. Others grab the body of the snail in their jaws and hold fast until the snail tires and its body can be pulled from the shell. These snakes typically track down snails and slugs by the mucous trails that they secrete as roadways over which to travel. Some snakes feed exclusively, or almost so, on crayfish. The queen snake of the eastern United States is one of them. Usually, it eats crayfish that have recently molted and are without the protection of a hard shell. The striped crayfish snake of Florida, on the other hand, is not so fastidious. It eats crayfish, hard shell and all.

Snakes have various hunting strategies. Some of them, such as ratsnakes, go actively on the prowl, rapidly searching nooks and crannies, both in the ground and in the trees, for prey. Others lie in ambush. The green body emerald tree boa of the American tropics enables it to hide among the foliage of the rain forest. It rests in a coil, its tail anchored to a branch. When a bird comes within striking distance, it launches the forward part of its body and seizes the prey in its jaws. The

53

massive bushmaster, a feared tropical American viper, has been observed waiting in ambush in places where rodents come to feed on seeds.

Defense, Defense

Snakes eat other animals. Many other animals eat snakes. Several birds are major predators of snakes. According to legend, the Aztecs decided to settle on what is now the site of Mexico City when they saw an eagle there with a rattlesnake clutched in its talons. Several species of hawks regularly prey on snakes. The secretary bird of Africa, which superficially resembles an eagle on stilts, stalks the plains on its long legs in search of snakes—and lizards—to eat. Some mammals will not turn down a snake dinner. Raccoons and skunks eat them. Pigs, wild and feral, will snap up a snake as they root around the ground for vegetable matter. Even frogs and toads sometimes turn the tables, gulping down small serpents.

So what's a poor snake to do to defend itself? Obviously, pythons and boas can use their muscles and savage bites. Venomous snakes defend themselves with chemical weaponry. So do some other snakes. Garter snakes and northern water snakes release foul-smelling, gooey secretion if roughly handled. Most snakes, though, would rather run than fight, and if threatened, they usually try to flee. Often, however, snakes rely on discretion. Their form and, frequently, color patterns, help them hide from danger, just as these qualities enable them to conceal them when they are after prey. When the emerald tree boa secretes itself in the foliage, it hides from enemies as well as from potential prey. The sidewinder that hunkers down in the sand escapes the sight of creatures that it would like to eat as well as those that would like to eat it. If disturbed, its rattle warns the interloper, "Don't tread on me." The racer, widely distributed in North America and sometimes called the "black snake," gives a good imitation of a rattlesnake to make aggressors think twice. It coils, makes bluff strikes and vibrates its tail, which in the dead leaves and other vegetation of the ground sounds like the buzz of a rattler. Expelled air, a hiss, if

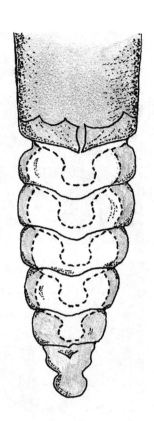

One of the most famous defense tactics belongs to the rattlesnake. The distinctive rattle at the end of its tail develops from scales. Young snakes have just a nub of a rattle, called a "button." Each rattle is shaped somewhat like a figure 8. New segments of the rattle are formed when the snake sheds, so older snakes have longer rattles than younger ones. The segments are brittle and loosely connected, however, and, with age, break off at the tip, so the old saw about counting a snake's rattles to calculate its age is not a truism. Specialized muscles in the tail vibrate the rattles and produce the characteristic buzzing sound.

you will, is another method by which snakes instinctively try to scare off enemies.

Bluff and bluster are a major defensive tactic of many snakes. Cobras do not rear up and spread their intimidating hoods when they are confronting prey. They do it when they are confronted by what they perceive to be danger. When it comes to bluff and bluster, the hognose snake of North America is a master. Perhaps no other allegedly harmless snake does a better imitation of one than is venomous than this eater of frogs and toads. When challenged, it copies from vipers and cobras. It puffs up its neck into a hood and hisses loudly. It coils and thrusts repeated strikes, although it does not make contact. Ironically, scientists have learned that this snake that was long deemed "non venomous," may have a mild venom that enables it to immobilize prey, but is not a true threat to humans.

A

B

The hognose snake tries bluff and bluster to frighten off enemies. If that tactic does not work, it feigns death.

C

LINDA KRULIKOWSKI

If the scary act of the hognose snake does not work, it tries another ploy. Like a frightened opossum, it plays dead. It flops over on its back, jaws open and tongue limply extended. It does indeed look dead—unless it is turned right side up again. Then it turns belly up and plays the roll again.

RED NEXT TO YELLOW

The coral snake, an elapid, lives along the southern Atlantic coast, and as far west as Texas, plus south into the tropics. It is a docile, retiring snake, but with highly toxic venom. Like a skunk, whose black-and-white fur warns people to steer clear of its noxious spray, the coral snake has what scientists term "warning coloration." Its body is ringed by alternating bands of red, yellow, and black in that order. One race of king snake, the scarlet, has a very similar color pattern, except that the black is between the red and the yellow. The distinction between the two Color patterns gives rise to the phrase, "Red next to yellow will kill a fellow." A number of other non-venomous North American snakes also protect themselves with similar mimicry.

CHAPTER 4

Increase and Multiply: How Snakes Spread and Diversified

Snakes are world citizens. They are found on all continents except Antarctica and most major—and many smaller—islands. Notable large islands with no native snakes are New Zealand, Iceland, Ireland—of course—Hawaii, and several other truly isolated islands of the central and south Pacific. Hawaii has one introduced snake, a miniscule burrowing species, and is now confronted with the possibility that the brown tree snake, a potentially dangerous species that has wrought havoc on Guam, may be accidentally introduced there.

Snakes have also colonized the ocean. Sea snakes and sea kraits are true marine animals. Sea kraits come ashore only to lay eggs. Sea snakes, virtually helpless on land, bear live young in the water. These snakes range the entire IndoPacific, but they are not found in the Atlantic. Since the Mesozoic era, the Age of Reptiles, when mosasaurs and pleisosaurs roamed the ocean, they are the only reptiles to live a fully marine existence, other than sea turtles. Well-known herpetologist Sherman A. Minton,

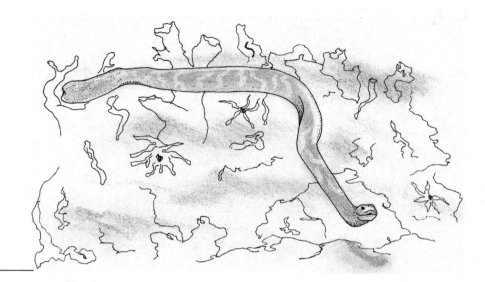

A sea snake winding through a coral reef.

in a paper presented in the book, *The Biology of Sea Snakes,* noted that, while some sea snakes venture into temperate waters, breeding is primarily carried on in tropical seas.

Home on the Range

The ranges of individual species and subspecies of snakes vary in scope, from spanning continents to holing up in areas the size of a country estate. The Round Island burrowing boa, a small snake that eats lizards, is confined to an islet in the Indian Ocean less than 300 acres in area. At the other end of the spectrum, the range of the Eurasian adder extends from Britain to Sakhalin Island, just off Far Eastern Russia in the Sea of Japan. It also is an Arctic explorer. It holds the distinction of being the only snake that lives north of the Arctic Circle. In northwestern Europe it has been found more than 100 miles deep within the Arctic. No other terrestrial snake has such a range, although many of them do cover considerable ground. The common garter snake, for example, inhabits most of the United States except for its southern quadrant, and ranges into the southern tier of Canada, one of the few snakes to go much farther north than the United States border.

The snake that contends with, and probably beats, the adder as the one with the most extensive range is the "pelagic" or, as it is often called, the "yellow-bellied" sea snake. It is aptly named. Other sea snakes stick to shallow seas. This one ranges the open ocean, often in immense groups, floating to the surface, wafted by wind and carried by waves and currents. Among sea snakes, it ventures where no sea snake has ever gone before. Here is a snake that can be found off Japan, in the South Pacific, the middle of ocean nowhere, and along the western shores of Central and South America, even close to Baja California. It is a blue-water sailor, while most other sea snakes are coastal cruisers.

Colonizing the World

Snakes, like the mammals that evolved before them, spread across the world because of the same forces that affect the dispersal of most other vertebrates. A host of factors, ranging from the drifting of continents to the presence or absence of competition for food and space, allow animals to disperse or hem them in, depending on the circumstances. A barrier to one animal, like water or a change in climate, can be a bridge to another.

Like the mammals that evolved before them, snakes appeared when the continents were close together, so tightly knit that they were joined in many places. (Eventually, due to continental drift, they would reach their present positions.) Snakes were able to fan out to the ends of the Earth, which were not nearly as far from one another then as they are now.

Even as the continents moved apart, and snakes were increasing in numbers and diversity, periodic drops in sea level created land bridges between continents and islands permitted continued spread of snakes. When colubrids evolved in Eurasia about 30 million years ago, for example, there was a huge bridge to North America, so this group of snakes spread there rapidly, in geologic terms. In their brave New World, once the continents were sundered, colubrids evolved into some species quite different than those of the Old. Still, some of the colubrids that emigrated to America maintain very close ties with their European cousins, even today. The Eurasian grass snake, a water snake that goes by the scientific name of *Natrix natrix*, is a look alike of America's northern water snake. Now known scientifically as *Nerodia sipedon*, the northern water snake was once, in the eyes of taxonomists, also *Natrix natrix*, which demonstrates that the two are virtually identical. As the colubrids advanced across Eurasia, the primitive boas, which had been widespread there, retreated before the advanced newcomers. Today, boas are numerous only in the American tropics and subtropics; only a handful of species, some primitive and isolated, remain in the Old World.

Barriers

Rattlesnakes, strictly a New World group, evolved in North America, which is still their citadel. Although there are many types of pit vipers in South America, there is only one rattlesnake. Why so? Scientists believed that by the time rattlesnakes diversified and began to move southward through Mexico, they ran into a significant barrier, the Isthmus of Panama. An isthmus can be what biogeographers call a "faunal corridor," a narrow zone that connects an animal's homeland with an area to which it may seem to migrate. This sort of corridor has less space and more restricted conditions than the land on either side, so fewer species can make a crossing successful enough to establish themselves across the way. In effect, the corridor filters out both individuals and species. What made the crossing of the Isthmus even more difficult for rattlesnakes was that about the time they may have tried it, rising sea levels were flooding the land link between the Americas. Only the brave, in this case the neotropical rattlesnake or its ancestors, survived the crossing.

Barriers not need be physical, such as water or high mountain ranges. Many other environmental factors can bar the way. In the case of snakes, cold is a major obstacle to expansion, perhaps the most daunting of all. The colder the climate, the fewer snakes exist. Snakes are absent, for example, from the southern tip of South America, where winter temperatures can be brutal. Their absence, however, may be due to lack of prey and cover as well as weather. Those few snakes that manage to live in colder regions have a highly restricted lifestyle. The Eurasian adders that live in the Arctic, for example, are active only for about a quarter of the year. The rest of the time they become dormant and den up. They must pack feeding, growth and reproduction into a few short months, activities that their conspecifics in southern Europe can leisurely extend through spring, summer and fall. Like most other snakes that live in the high latitudes, the adder bears live young, obviating the need for heat to incubate eggs. It is also dark in color, enabling it to soak up the sun's heat more efficiently. In the northeastern and upper midwestern United States, the black rat snake, for the same reason, is one of the first species to emerge from its winter dens.

No better example exists of how cold temperatures can deter snakes from expanding than the reason why sea snakes, which apparently evolved in the IndoPacific, have not migrated to the tropical Atlantic, despite millions of years available in which to do it. The South Atlantic and the IndoPacific meet at Cape of Good Hope on the Southern tip of Africa, and at Cape Horn, which reaches from South America towards the Antarctic. However, sea snakes, powerful swimmers that they are, have not made the passage. Sea snakes seem to need temperatures of at least 68°F. to survive for any long period of time. The temperature of the water around both capes, chilled by flow from the Antarctic, is well below this level.

Snakes and the Ice Ages

Sometimes physical and environmental barriers team up to influence the distribution of snakes. In his book *The Snakes of Europe*, British herpetologist J. W. Steward offers a concise explanation that Europe's paucity of snake species—less than three dozen, compared to more than 100 in the United States and 300 in Mexico—is largely a result of Pleistocene glaciation. He also explains how glaciation may have caused many species of European snakes—vipers, for instance—to split up into several subspecies.

At its maximum, the ice extended as far south as northern Germany, European Russia, and England. South of the glacial margin tundra, cold grasslands and taiga, too chilly for snakes, stretched across Central Europe. Glaciers also expanded on the Alps and Pyrenees, sealing off southern Italy and Spain. Only in these two areas along with the Balkans did the climate remain moderate enough, because of the Mediterranean's influence, to support deciduous forest—and snakes.

Glaciation decimated Europe's reptile species. Some species of snakes, although not many, found refuge in the Mediterranean enclaves. Cut off from each other in these refuges, members of the same species well may have differentiated into subspecies. After the last glaciation, some, although by no means all, of the refugees left their enclaves and spread out across Europe. The climate was warmer then than it is today so some species, such as the Aesculapian snake, penetrated far into the north. As temperatures dropped to a more typical level, this species retreated to Central and Southern Europe, where it lives today. Meanwhile, species more tolerant of cold, such as the adder, expanded their ranges due to limited competition.

Why There Are No Snakes in Ireland

Saint Patrick did not have a difficult job chasing snakes from Ireland. There were not any there. Ireland and Britain were almost completely glaciated. The low sea level allowed land bridges to connect them and link Britain with the continent. After the ice melted, some 12,000 years ago, the bridge to Ireland was quickly inundated. But the English Channel was not flooded until almost 8,000 years ago. A few snakes managed to get from Europe to Britain before the breach; Britain has three species. None made it to Ireland.

Island Hopping

Most snakes are adept swimmers, although not in the sea snake's long-distance mode. How then, did snakes get to islands? One way, as in the case of Britain's snakes and those of the Aegean Islands, is to use land bridges when sea level is down, and islands are not yet islands. Existing islands are another matter. The main route taken by snakes is called "rafting."

Scientists believe that snakes, as well as many other animals, colonize islands, both near and far flung, by sailing across the sea on logs, roots, and other types of vegetative flotsam washed into the water. Reptiles are ideal rafters because they can go for long periods without food or drink. Still, it is no easy task. A rafter snake is at the mercy of wind, waves, and current. If it does get to land, it needs proper habitat to survive. Even if it has the right conditions for living at its new destination, how does it reproduce? That is the rub. The chances of a male and female snake arriving on the right island at the right time to reproduce approach lottery odds. Nevertheless, it apparently happens. Even greater are the odds that a female, laden with eggs or young, will make a landfall before she is ready to produce offspring and in a place where the young will find food and proper living conditions. Nevertheless, it apparently happens in this case, too.

There is another way that snakes, and many other animals, have voyaged to new homes. It is by hitchhiking with traveling humans.

Hitching a Ride

Hawaii had no pigs or rats before the sea-faring Polynesians arrived there more than 1500 years ago. Once humans hit the Hawaiian beach, both animals became residents of the islands. The first human settlers of the Hawaiian Islands brought pigs with them on purpose and the rats stowed away on their seagoing canoes. Some of the pigs went wild, as they have done in the southern United States, where they are called "razorbacks." The rats ran rampant across the islands, as rats are wont to do. Both pigs and rats destroyed many native species. Introduced species often create havoc because they have no native predators or competitors to stop their spread.

Hawaii had no snakes until a few decades ago when a tiny blind snake native to India landed there in the soil of potted plants, thus, it's common name, the "flower pot snake." Native to India, the flower-pot snake has spread world wide, to places as far apart as Australia and Florida. It has been able to establish itself because it is the ultimate feminist. It is one of a few reptile species composed solely of females. The females are partheno-genetic, which means that they produce fertile eggs without the help of a male. The flower-pot snake, as far as we know, has not done any damage to the ecology of the areas in which it has been introduced.

Invasion of the Brown Tree Snake

For several years, Hawaii has been on the alert to guard against the accidental introduction of another snake, which is far from harmless. It is the brown tree snake, native to eastern Indonesia, the Solomon Islands, New Guinea and northern and eastern Australia. Reaching a length of about nine feet, the brown tree snake was inadvertently brought to Guam, 3800 miles southwest of Hawaii, in the cargo of military vessels during the late 1940s. In the absence of natural controls such as predators (feral pigs do kill some of the snakes, but not many), the tree snake reproduced and swarmed over the island. Some areas of Guam's low forest have up to 13,000 tree snakes per square mile.

The tree snake has virtually wiped out forest birds on Guam. Twelve species of birds, including several native only to Guam, have disappeared since the snake arrived. The snake also poses a threat to very young children. It is a rear-fanged species with mild venom, and is of minimal danger to adults; but it has attacked sleeping infants, apparently in an attempt to eat them. The snake wraps its powerful body around its prey, holding it fast while chewing in venom, so the possibility of strangulation as well as envenomation of in-fants is very real. The tree snake also has caused more than a thousand power outages, a result of its penchant for crawling on utility lines.

Since the late 1980s, a handful of individual brown tree snakes have been caught on Hawaii, and others have been found on islands ranging from Saipan to Okinawa. And one of the snakes was found at Corpus Christi, Texas. Perhaps by luck, the snake has become established only on Guam, because some of those captured on Hawaii were pregnant females. Hawaiian authorities have mounted an extensive surveillance and trapping campaign as precautions against the snake arriving in cargo from Guam. An element of the campaign might be called the "canine connection." Feisty Jack Russell terriers are used in Guam to nose out, and often kill, snakes that might be in outgoing cargo. At the Hawaiian end, snake-sniffing beagles check out incoming shipments.

SOME NATIVE ISLAND SNAKES

Species	Island	Sea or Ocean
• Round Island boa (Bolyeria multicarinata)	Round Island, Mauritius,	Indian (note: perhaps extinct)
• Round Island burrowing boa (Casarea dussumieri)	"	"
• Seychelles wolf snake (Lycognathophis seychellensis)	Seychelles	"
• Nasuta vine snake (Langaha nasuta)	Madagascar	"
• Jamaican boa (Epicrates subflavus)	Jamaica	Caribbean
• Antiguan racer	Antigua	" (note: now confined to Great Bird Island)
• Fer-de-Lance (Bothrops lancelatus)	Martinique	"
• Okinawa habu (Trimeresurus flavoviridis)	Okinawa and Anami Islands, Japan	Pacific
• Fiji snake (Ogmodon vitianus)	Viti Levu, Fiji	"

CHAPTER 5

Snake Country

S nakes, along with their ancestors, the lizards, live in a far greater variety of habitats than any other reptiles. It is a wonder that these legless creatures, dependent upon their surroundings to keep themselves from freezing or overheating, can live from forests where it freezes in winter to the tropics; from beneath the soil, in the sea, to the treetops.

The extent of a snake's range does not necessarily reflect whether or not it is restricted to one or more types of habitat. As noted, sea snakes rove a vast portion of the globe. But their habitat is confined to oceans. They could not survive on land. The Eurasian adder, with the largest land range of any snake, does very well in a wide variety of habitats, including open woods, hedgerows, rocky hillsides, wooded steppes, moors, and even sandy areas and swamps. However, it needs relatively natural conditions and retreats from areas that have been taken over by agriculture, not to mention more intensive development. Changes in the natural environment created by humans are not always detrimental to snakes. A farm pond on the dry high plains of the American West can benefit garter snakes because it attracts frogs, toads and other amphibians, and contains fish, all of which are mainstays of the snake's diet. Canals, while they may drain wetland habitat attractive to aquatic snakes, also furnish them with fish and amphibians, as well as corridors through which they can travel to new hunting grounds. Two types of habitat, desert and tropical forest, are especially useful to snakes, and it is in these environments that snakes reach their greatest diversity.

Deserts

Snakes have exploited deserts because they eat less frequently than, for instance, mammals and birds. This is due partly to the fact that external warmth, rather than oxidation of food, heats their bodies. Certainly, there is heat enough in deserts, although in cold deserts, such as that of the Great Basin of the western United States, temperatures can go below 0°F. in winter. Snakes there respond to the chill just as do snakes in other areas with cold winters; they hibernate. Moreover, in a desert, as elsewhere, snakes possess behaviors that enable them to control their body temperature. When they need warmth, they get a few rays by exposing their bodies to the sun or to a warm substrate, like a rock that has been heated by the sun. Because rocks retain heat for considerable periods of time, they serve as hot pockets for snakes that need warmth as the sun goes down. Cooling off under the scorching desert sun is not much of a problem for a snake. Their long bodies expose little surface to the sun—and enable them to creep into a crack, cranny, or burrow out of the heat.

Snakes also are particularly efficient at water conservation. It is not only a matter of the way that their scales slow the evaporation of water from their bodies; like other creatures, they must rid their bodies of ammonia through body waste. Their waste is composed of uric acid, a semi solid containing a minimal amount of water.

Many small desert rodents, such as kangaroo mice, have a similar means of conserving water when they eliminate waste. While large mammals are few and far between in deserts, rodents are common. They forage for food in the cool of the night, which means that the darkness is prime-time hunting for snakes, especially for American pit vipers, whose heat-sensitive organs can track down prey in the darkness. It should not be surprising that pit vipers are among the most numerous snakes of North American deserts. Many desert pit vipers, such as the sidewinder rattlesnake, have stout, squat bodies, adapted for pushing away sand as they travel via sideways loops. Other desert snakes, such as the shovel-nosed snake, travel beneath the sand using the "S-curve" that most snakes employ above the ground. The snake's spadelike snout, from which it gets its name, helps it shove aside sand particles.

Tropical Forests

Tropical forests, especially rain forests, have the greatest diversity of life of any land habitat. (Their counterpart in the sea is the coral reef.) Like the coral reef, the tropical forest is the home of an incredible number of animal species, but not immense populations of any one of them. For snakes, the tropical forest is like a smorgasbord. It has a wide variety of food offerings. Snakes that are generalists as feeders can pick and choose. On the other hand, tropical forests gave so many different forms of animal prey that many snakes living there have adapted to specialized diets.

The tropical forest has many ecological niches for snakes, arranged vertically between the forest floor and the top of the canopy of trees, some of which are more than 200 feet high. From top to bottom the tropical forest has several vegetative zones, or *strata*. Some animals range up and down through several, even all of these zones. Others stick to a few, or even only one, of them. The stratification of the forest makes it rather like an apartment building for animals. The typical tropical forest has five layers, six if you count the soil beneath the floor.

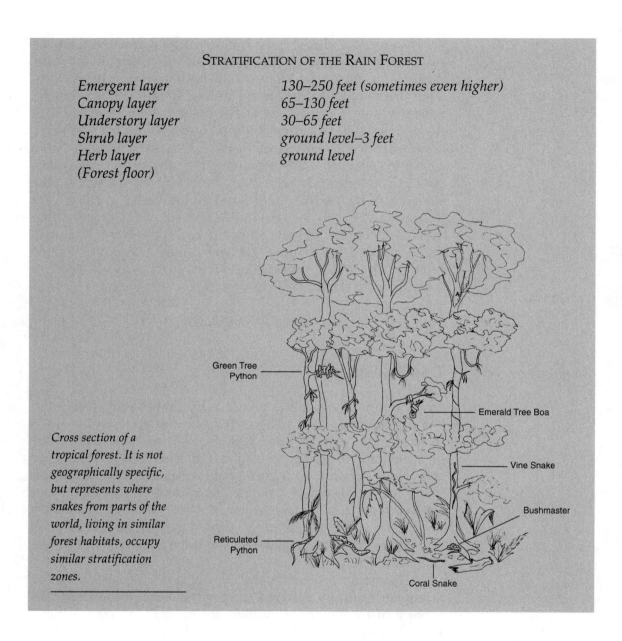

STRATIFICATION OF THE RAIN FOREST

Emergent layer	*130–250 feet (sometimes even higher)*
Canopy layer	*65–130 feet*
Understory layer	*30–65 feet*
Shrub layer	*ground level–3 feet*
Herb layer	*ground level*
(Forest floor)	

Green Tree
Python

Emerald Tree Boa

Vine Snake

Bushmaster

Reticulated
Python

Coral Snake

Cross section of a tropical forest. It is not geographically specific, but represents where snakes from parts of the world, living in similar forest habitats, occupy similar stratification zones.

Some forest snakes, such as the boa constrictor, hunt from the forest floor up to the understory. The boa constrictor can climb but cannot be considered truly arboreal, and the bigger it grows, the less it can negotiate small tree limbs. Others, like the green mamba of Africa, are at least partly arboreal, and there are many species that spend virtually their entire lives in the branches; as high up as the canopy. The canopy of a tropical forest, seen from above, looks solid, and almost is. Some of the crowns of canopy trees are an acre in expanse. Huge vines, some as long as a modern jetliner and as thick as a man's torso, lace through the branches, connecting one tree with another.

Not surprisingly, high-living canopy snakes feed largely on birds. Among the latter are the vine snakes, tree boas, and some tree pythons. Typically, snakes that live in the branches have long, slender bodies and are green in color, like the vine snakes of both the Old and New World. The configuration of their bodies and color are superb camouflage, which helps them catch prey and protects them from becoming such. Many arboreal snakes, moreover, have prehensile tails that anchor them to branches.

One group of arboreal snakes in southern Asia is remarkable for their ability to go airborne. These so-called "flying snakes" are really gliders, or parachutists. These snakes spread and tuck their bodies so that their underside is concave, then launch themselves into the air and sail softly to the ground.

The forest floor supports a host of snakes, including vipers, such as West Africa's feared Gaboon viper, which blends in to fallen leaves, and various small, fossorial snakes that burrow into the earth and live on invertebrates such as termites, ants and worms.

The ability of a flying snake to glide comes from its flexible ribs, which arch out and spread its body into parachute shape, above.

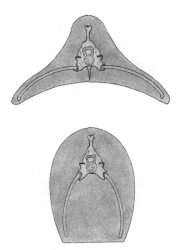

CONVERGENT EVOLUTION

Convergent evolution is the name scientists use for creatures that are unrelated, or almost so, and often geographically far apart, yet have developed similar adaptations for survival. The classic and often cited example of this phenomenon is set by two snakes, the emerald tree boa of the American tropics and the green tree python of northern Australia, New Guinea and neighboring areas. Both are about five feet long, with bodies that are relatively slender for boids. As boids, they are related but quite distantly. Boas, as noted earlier, bear live young, while pythons lay eggs, evidence that they are far from close kin. Both snakes are green as the leaves in which they hide. They catch prey in the same manner. Anchored to a limb by the rear portion of their body, they let the fore body hang downwards, as if it were a vine. When a bird comes in reach, the head shoots out and the jaws clasp the victim. Though they are half a world apart, both survive the same way in the world of the canopy. What works for one, works for the other.

Temperate Forests

Temperate forests of deciduous and mixed deciduous-conifers are not nearly as hospitable to snakes as those of the tropics. These forests are stratified, but far less vegetated, and the zones are less defined. It is much easier for a snake to reach the canopy of a thickly woven tropical forest than it is in a temperate forest. Snakes are relatively uncommon in the deep, temperate woodlands. Those that do live in this environment, such as copperheads, timber rattlesnakes, and some racers, often seek out rocky hillsides, clearings, and edges between forest and field. In such areas, they find sunlight for warmth. Tropical forest snakes, living in temperatures well above the Temperate Zone, are not nearly as dependent upon the sun's heat. In suitable temperate forest habitat, such as rocky ledges facing south, those species that inhabit the forest, such as copperheads, may be locally quite common.

This is not to say that all thickly wooded areas in temperate climate are bereft of snakes. Some, such as the dry flatwoods of Florida, where scrubby pines grow in sandy soil, are well-suited to certain snakes. Eastern diamondback rattlesnakes, for example, have a home in the flatwoods. Compared to the dense forests of New England and the Upper Midwest, however, the piney woods of the Southeast, relatively unshaded and baked by the sun in summer, can be considered as open woodlands of a type quite different from forests to the north.

Grasslands

Both temperate and tropical grasslands of the world have been largely changed by agriculture and stock raising. By and large, these activities have been harmful to snakes although, as noted earlier, the creation of farm ponds and hedgerows sometimes enhance habitat for certain species. Because grasslands do not have a large variety of ecological niches, wildlife there is not particularly diverse, although in the case of large species of mammals the numbers of individuals can be monumental. Consider the fact that 60 million bison once roamed the grasslands of North America.

Most of the snakes that inhabit grasslands, including the pine snakes, racers, rat snakes, the coachwhip snakes, and hognose snakes, are also found in other habitats, particularly partly open ones such as desert scrub and pine barrens.

Freshwater Wetlands, Streams, and Ponds

Many snakes associate themselves with marshes, swamps and other freshwater wetlands, as well as streams and standing bodies of water, especially those with wetlands on their fringes. Only a few are totally aquatic. Among these are the wart snakes,

CITY CRITTERS
Urbanization does not sound the death knell for all snakes. Various cobras in Asia haunt towns, seeking out rats and other rodents in homes and granaries. The little brown snake, which manages in multiple habitats, thrives on golf courses, city parks and even among the rubble of vacant lots in Manhattan. In the city it has fewer predators during its search for snails, slugs, and other small invertebrates upon which it feeds.

named for their rough scales, which live from southern Asia to Australia. Like sea snakes, they are virtually helpless on land.

Snakes that make use of the water as feeding grounds are legion. They range from the great anaconda of the American tropics to garter snakes. Wetlands not only provide food, but plenty of vegetative cover, from the thickets of swamps to the floating vegetation of marshes. The water itself can be a place of concealment. Anacondas often lie by the water's edge, submerged but for eyes and nostrils, waiting for terrestrial prey, such as capybaras and deer, to drink. A quick lunge by the anaconda, and the prey is dragged into the water and dispatched.

CHAPTER 6

Here There Be Giants

Godzilla aside, some living reptiles grow to breathtaking size. Saltwater crocodiles of Australia, New Guinea and adjacent areas, reach more than 25 feet in length. The leatherback sea turtle can grow to more than 10 feet long and 1600 pounds. Big, yes, but even these reptiles do not capture the human imagination as the tales of monstrous, giant serpents; beasts of prodigious proportions, longer than a railway car, powerful beyond belief. These snakes lurk in hidden enclaves of the imagination and, perhaps, of the wild, a symbol of the power that reptiles held when the mammalian ancestors of our kind were the size of rats and confined to the shadows. Do such giant snakes really exist in today's world? There is some tantalizing evidence that they may.

Giants, Real and Imagined

For decades, the Wildlife Conservation Society, formerly known as the New York Zoological Society, has offered a substantial cash reward for the receipt of a live snake that can be accurately measured as more than 30 feet in length. No one has ever claimed it. The reward was not established solely to obtain a huge snake for exhibit and the attendant media attention, but mainly in the interests of science. Despite myriad stories about snakes as long as fire hoses, no live snake longer than 30 feet has ever been measured to the acceptance of the scientific community.

During the early 1990s, a group of businessmen in Borneo thought that they had a chance at the prize. They were traders in snake leather; snake skin makes attractive boots, belts, pocketbooks and clothing. Prowling the forest, their hunters had caught a mighty reticulated python. The word "reticulated" derives from the Latin name for "net," referring to the net-like markings on python's skin. (In the Roman arena, the gladiator who used a fisherman's net, trident and dagger to battle his opponents was called a "retiarius," a "net man.")

The leather traders decided that the python might be a candidate for the zoo's award. After months of negotiation, during which the python was confined within a railroad boxcar in Borneo, the snake finally arrived at the Bronx Zoo. She—turned out to be a female—was skinny from a poor captive diet. She weighed only 150 pounds, two-thirds of the weight of a healthy snake of her length, which turned out to be 21 feet. Although she fell far short of the 30-foot mark, leaving the leather traders very disappointed, a snake 21 feet long is still an impressive animal. It is, in fact, a true giant. Today, fed and cared for by the zoo, "Samantha," as she is known, has prospered at the zoo. Within a few years of arriving there, she weighed upwards of 250 pounds and was 24 feet long and counting, as far as was known, longer than any other snake in captivity.

The fact that no one has been able to claim the reward offered by the Bronx Zoo, now known as the Wildlife Conservation Park, does not prove that no snakes surpass 30 feet in length. To the contrary, there is plenty of evidence that some may, although most of it unsupported by severe scientific scrutiny, that such creatures may indeed exist.

All of the truly giant snakes are either boas or pythons. They include the anaconda, an aquatic South America boid; the reticulated python of Southeast Asia; the African rock python; the scrub (or amethystine) python of Australia and New Guinea; the Indian python of southern Asia; and the boa constrictor of the American tropics. Of these, the big two are the anaconda and reticulated python. Even if no one has a live specimen to prove it, many professional herpetologists would agree that unusual representatives of these two species might surpass 30 feet. By how much is debatable. The anaconda is by far the heavier of the two, so generally is recognized as the best candidate for the world's largest snake. An anaconda of 20 feet or so can weigh as much as a reticulated python six or seven feet longer.

The African rock python can grow to perhaps 25 feet, the scrub python almost as large, and the Indian python to about 20 feet. The boa constrictor can reach a length of 18 feet, but that is a truly gargantuan individual. Indeed, a 12-foot boa constrictor is considered a whopper. Some venomous snakes can also grow to considerable lengths. Notable among them is the king cobra, which can be as long as the biggest boa constrictors. So big can the cobra grow that several years ago two golfers on a course in Singapore grabbed what they thought was a python and brought their captive for their friends to see, causing a considerable ruckus because it was actually a king cobra that, for some reason, failed to deliver a venomous bite. The eastern diamondback rattlesnake, an inhabitant of lowlands in the southeastern United States, and a creature that often enters salt water, can also grow to considerable bulk. Considered the most dangerous snake in the country, this creature can reach a length of eight feet in extreme cases. (Rumors persist amidst residents of the Florida Everglades that a few diamondbacks may be even longer.) While the length of the eastern diamondback is not astonishing, it is known for its impressive bulk. The following story illustrates that fact.

Tom Brelsford is a veteran conservation officer for the State of Connecticut. He spent his boyhood living at the edge of the Everglades. The area around his home, he relates, was eastern diamondback country. He and his family frequently saw the snakes. Near the edge of the yard some old tires had been piled.

One day, Brelsford's mother asked him why a tire had been moved into the middle of the yard. Young Brelsford looked outside the house and realized that the "tire" was not what his mother had thought it to be. It was a coiled diamondback.

Much of my information on giant snakes derives from my close friend and mentor, the late Dr. James A. Oliver, one of the world's most respected herpetologists before he died in the late 1970s. We were working on a book about his life at the time, and he offered much information about giant snakes during conversations and in typewritten manuscripts that added to and elaborated upon his highly popular book, *Snakes in Fact and Fiction* (The Macmillan Company, 1958). Jim Oliver was not only a superb researcher of reptiles. He also held major positions in the zoo and museum field. Oliver was curator of reptiles at the Bronx Zoo, director of the zoo, director of the American Museum of Natural History and, towards the end of his career, director of the New York Aquarium. I knew him since the early 1960s, when he headed the museum while I worked there during a graduate fellowship at Columbia University.

Oliver was every inch a scientist and, as great scientists often are, he usually was quite conservative when it came to making scientific pronouncements without solid evidence. Nevertheless, he promulgated a belief that, by his admission, many of his colleagues in the field of herpetology considered a myth. Based upon historical accounts, unconfirmed reports from other scientists, communications from various people around the world, and his deep understanding on snakes, Oliver became convinced that, possibly in remote areas, there lurked anacondas and reticulated pythons that were goliaths indeed. In Oliver's opinion, reticulated pythons up to 33 feet long were highly likely. As for anacondas, he suggested that they could be considerably longer, 37 feet perhaps, and possibly, he hinted, even larger than that.

Stories from the Bush

Oliver closely studied historical and recent accounts of people who had seen and/or captured huge snakes. On July 13, 1956, a geologist for the government of French Guiana replied to a letter that Oliver, then running the Bronx Zoo's reptile department, had written him a few months earlier. The letter from the geologist, a Dutch scientist named Dr. Henk Cruys, follows in abridged form.

"I am very sorry to be so long in answering your letter of Mai 22. However, I have been nearly two months in the bush, up the Marowijne River . . .

I am very glad to be able to give you some information about large anacondas, killed here in French Guiana, as far as I know. . . .

In the beginning of this year—in February—one of my French prospectors, Mr. Tartaroli—a very good hunter— killed two large anacondas—one with a length of 8 meters and the other slightly longer. . . . Both snakes were killed in the Sparouine Creek, a right tributary of the great Marowinjne River. . . . The anaconda with a length of 8 m. was a female, bearing twenty-seven little snakes [anacondas bear live young], each of about 50 centimeters long. These little snakes had two different skin colors (sexual differentiation?). The largest anaconda was busy to digest a so-called "pakira" [peccary] with a weight of 30 kilograms. We preserved both skins. One skin was given to Mr. Secher, physician in Saint Jean [a small village]. Unfortunately, the other skin is now in bad condition. Enclosed you will find a photo of one of these skins . . .

Moreover, Mr. Tartaroli told me that, four years ago, he killed already a much larger anaconda: 11 meters long! This beast—"full up" with scales of the large "aymara" fish and with remnants of the agouti, a rodent species—was killed in the Laussat Creek, near the road—very bad road— from Organabo to St. Sabbat. . . . Considering this last giant snake, I like to notice that Mr. Tartaroli is a very reliable man, who does not like to tell untrue stories and incorrect facts. . . ."

The story told by Cruys is an echo of myriad similar reports about giant snakes that have filtered down over the years. Oliver was told by Henry Trefflich, a legendary and legitimate animal dealer who supplied zoos worldwide, that he had personally measured a recticulated python of 32 feet. In 1931, Raymond L. Ditmars, a predecessor of Oliver's as the Bronx Zoo's reptile curator, and whose popular writing on serpents drew world-wide attention, proclaimed that the reticulated python could reach the 33-foot mark. His opinion was not supported by cold scientific evidence but upon his knowledge of snakes in general. To give it credence, Ditmars remains revered today by herpetologists as one of the pioneers and giants of the field.

Because of their jaw structure and elastic bodies, snakes can consume prey of incredible bulk relative to their size, although the meals that snakes consume are not always as huge as exist in the popular imagination. There are countless stories of large anacondas and pythons swallowing creatures as large as cattle and deer. Many are true, but the victims generally were not massive examples of their species. These snakes can swallow small or young antelope or deer, in the 50-to-100 pound range. Sometimes, the prey can be even larger, perhaps up to 150 pounds. Despite the anaconda's reputation as a "bull killer," a domestic calf is a much more manageable meal. It is unusual for a python or anaconda to gulp down a pig, wild or domestic, weighing in the neighborhood of 100 pounds, give or take a few.

How Dangerous Are Large Snakes?

Unquestionably, a large anaconda or python can overpower and swallow an adult human. However, there are only a handful of accounts suggesting that these snakes may prey on people. Most involve reticulated pythons. James Oliver, in his book *Snakes in Fact and Fiction*, cites one report of a hunter swallowed by a large python in Burma and another of a woman eaten by a python in the East Indies. Generally, however, the few attacks by giant snakes in humans are in the defensive mode. Pythons and anacondas can bite viciously with their recurved teeth and have inflicted severe wounds on people, mostly in a captive situation. However, it is their coils that are to be feared most, as proven by a case in New York City in 1996. Two teenage brothers kept a Burmese python as a pet. One of the boys frequently draped the snake around his neck. It was a bad policy. The boy, who had been alone with the snake, was found dead. Authorities deduced that the snake had coiled around the youth's neck and strangled him.

The writings of J. J. Quelch, a prominent naturalist who studied constrictor snakes in British Guiana during the 1890s, add to the speculation that monster anacondas may exist. He declared that the anaconda can reach a length of 37 feet and that even larger specimens have been reported. In 1894, Quelch had an up-close-and-personal encounter with an anaconda that, upon reading it, can send the proverbial chills down the spine. Quelch was navigating a swampy river by boat. His craft was passing through a heavy growth of aquatic vegetation near the bank—a perfect place for a water-loving serpent to hide. The movement of the boat, he reported, "disturbed an enormous snake." The creature was only five feet away. It's head was colossal, Quelch said, "more than twice as large as that of one about twenty feet." This observation, he noted, indicated that the snake was of "very large proportions."

Quelch noted, however, that he would not place his reputation on the line by certifying that anacondas reach lengths of 37 feet and more. ". . . unless definite measurements are made, the estimate of size can be of little value."

Snakes of gigantic size are of considerable age, because serpents never stop growing. The absolute life span of giant snakes in the wild is uncertain. However, snakes can have a respectable lifespan. Some cobras and rattlesnakes have lived for a score or more years. Anacondas and pythons have the potential to live for much longer than that.

EAT OR BE EATEN

Even the giant snakes are not immune to predation. Small anacondas are meals for caimans and some of the giant catfish that inhabit the Amazon and its tributaries. Crocodiles will eat young pythons that venture into the streams of Africa, Asia and Australia. Certainly, herons and other large birds frequently sup on the very young of the giants. Hawks, eagles and, in Africa, secretary birds—which feast on snakes—have no respect for a stripling snake that, if it grows to maturity could gulp them down with the gusto of an NFL lineman eating a steak. It is a question of eat or be eaten. And, from my own experience, the difference between who eats and who is supper may not always depend on the size of the snake. During the seventies, on my first of many assignments in Africa, I was in the field with the warden of Kenya's Nakuru National Park. We had approached a small, swift stream, perhaps a dozen feet across and a yard or so deep at most. Alongside the stream was

a large group of marabou storks, big birds, five feet tall, with long, powerful bills. They were hunting for frogs, which they consume in volumes when they cannot share carrion with the omnipresent vultures.

The warden surveyed the stream, then looked at me and made a gesture for me to be silent. Then he pointed towards the water. There, amidst the foam where the current broached a natural dam of rocks, I saw a large, triangular head. It belonged to a rock python. With its body obscured by the water, an estimate of its size was difficult to make, but it was at least a dozen feet long, probably more. It was eyeing the storks and fighting the current so it could approach them. It moved slowly, not only because of the water's resistance, but to maintain its concealment. After several minutes, it neared the bank, a few yards from the storks. There, it froze. Too late. The storks had seen the snake. Instead of fleeing, as I had expected they might, they clustered together and edged towards the bank. Their eyes were all turned towards the snake. A careful step at a time, they came closer. I realized that a drama was ensuing that could end with the tables—dinner tables, that is— turning. The storks, as a group, were considering the python as a meal. As the storks neared the water's edge, the snake withdrew its head under the surface and let the current bring it downstream. It was the better part of valor.

Measuring Snakes

And measuring large snakes, alive or dead, is no easy task. Taking the measure of a skin that has been lifted from a dead snake is often inaccurate, because during the process of stripping the hide from the carcass, the skin may stretch to a quarter more than its live length. When it comes to a big anaconda, python, or boa constrictor that is alive and kicking, the process is even more difficult. Even a dozen strong people cannot straighten out one of these beasts without kinks. It is like trying to uncoil concertina wire. I had a boa constrictor of about 10 feet for many years. Even with a little help from my friends, I could never get it to totally stretch out. During my days at the Bronx Zoo, I assisted reptile department staffers in handling big pythons and anacondas on a few occasions. The resistance that I felt from the muscles of these creatures seemed as if it were drawn from the basic strength of the Earth. It was the first anaconda I handled— I am talking about a lowly 15-footer—that was the most awesome. After I helped handle it for the first time I made a note in my journal that it seemed as if I was holding "liquid steel." The intrinsic power of such a snake—reptile experts in zoos would vouch for it—is daunting and absolute. There is no doubt in my mind that even under the controlled conditions of a zoo it is exceedingly difficult to measure the length of a large snake down to the exact inch.

Thus it is that there is no universally accepted record of a snake more than 30 feet long. Even so, it is possible that somewhere out in the tropical bush and forests lurk giants of their kind that are the stuff of which legends are made.

C H A P T E R   7

The Poisoners

Human fear of serpents is engendered almost entirely by those species that can deliver a venomous bite. It is somewhat ironic that even among the snakes which can, only a minority can cause severe damage to humans and even fewer qualify as man-killers. Some of those that are in this last category, however, are downright fearsome. The venom of some cobras and rattlesnakes, for example, is 30,000 times more potent than strychnine. Sea snake venom is also notoriously toxic, perhaps more so than that of rattlesnakes or cobras. Snake venom retains its toxicity, sometimes for scores of years. It is a highly evolved biochemical weapon.

Snake venom is a modified form of saliva. Venom is a clear, viscous liquid, tinged with yellow in viperids and elpaids, colorless in colubrids. In vipers, pit vipers, and elapids it is produced by a pair of glands similar to salivary glands in humans and many other animals. Each gland is covered with a muscular sheath of connective tissue that contracts when venom is discharged. From the gland, the venom flows through a duct to the

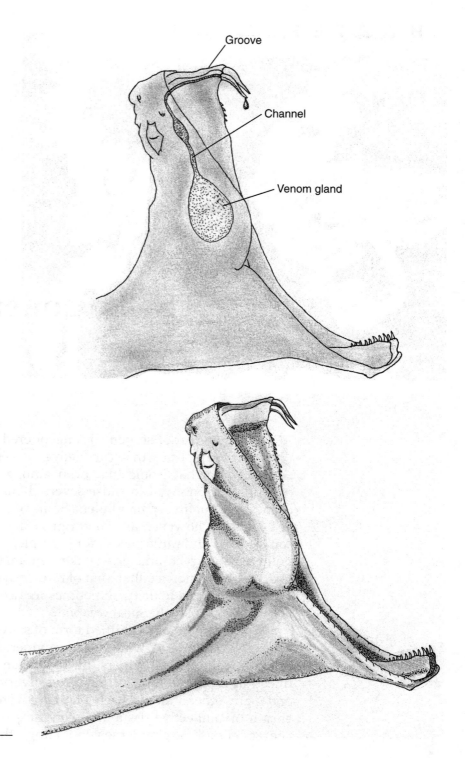

Groove

Channel

Venom gland

The gape of a rattlesnake's jaws when striking is enormous. Unlike the cobra, the rattlesnake does not bite, it stabs. Note the powerful muscles in the jaw, the venom gland and its channel to the fangs, and the ejection of venom.

The venom glands of the Malaysian long-glanded coral snake, an elapid, extend from its head one-third the length of its body.

LINDA KRULIKOWSKI

fangs, located in the front of the upper jaw, which introduce the toxin into the victim. Glands, ducts, and fangs are known scientifically as the "venom apparatus."

The venomous colubrids, such as the African boomslang, have a different arrangement. They lack true venom glands. Instead, their venom comes from the Duvernoy's gland on the upper angle of the rear hinge on each side of the jaw. This gland is composed of tissue similar to that of dental enamel. Venom seeps from the gland through a duct that empties at the base of fangs in the rear of the upper jaw. Some venomous colubrids—again, the boomslang is a prime example—have two venom-introducing fangs on each side of the rear upper jaw. Snakes with fangs in this position, whether or not venomous, are known as rear-fanged snakes. The mole vipers have a similar apparatus, except that their fangs are in the side of the jaw.

The action that triggers the discharge of venom is not related to the mechanisms of biting so the snake can actually regulate the amount of venom it releases. It can deliver a dose from one or more fangs, or from neither. Some studies indicate that venomous snakes may frequently hold back their toxic weaponry when in a defensive posture. According to a manual on venomous snakes issued in 1962 by the Department of the Navy for Naval and Marine personnel, and produced by a committee of leading herpetologists of the day, between three and 40 percent of bites inflicted by venomous snakes, no signs of poisoning develop. Seldom does a snake evacuate all of the venom in its glands. Rattlesnakes probably eject between 25 and 75 percent of their venom when they strike a human. Elapids, the most varied family of venomous snakes, also vary extremely in the amount of venom they eject.

In Case of Snakebite

Snakebite victims today have a far better chance of surviving even the most dangerous venoms than in the past—if, that is, they are treated quickly and if medical facilities are available. Many snakebite remedies of yesteryear—even if, by luck, they appeared to have worked—were counter productive and, indeed, decreased the chances of a victim's survival. Erroneous notions about the proper way to treat snakebite were once accepted by even experts on reptiles. The following notice to keepers was posted in the Bronx Zoo's Reptile House on December 26, 1899, by Raymond L. Ditmars, who was one of the world's top reptile authorities of his time. His writings on reptiles are still treasured by people who study these creatures.

In Case of Snakebite

"Should a bite be received on the hand, arm or leg, immediately follow the instructions here given:

1. Plunge a knife into the punctures slightly DEEPER than the fang wounds. Repeat the operation across the first cut, making the incision thus: —/—.

2. Call for assistance.

3. Suck the wound, spitting the blood out frequently. Use the teeth to draw the blood towards the injury.

4. Have a ligature tied above the injured part. The same should be tightened with a stick.

5. Continue sucking the wound until the blood practically ceases to flow.

6. Have a second ligature placed about the first without removing the latter.

7. If the bite be from one of the larger snakes have a physician summoned.

8. Rinse out the mouth with a weak solution of Permanganate Potash. (In office) Wash the wound thoroughly with the same solution.

9. Take a full wineglass of whisky. NO MORE.

10. DON'T remove ligatures until so advised by surgical authority.

"NOTE: With proper caution an accident is practically impossible. Our motto should be: "GREATER CAUTION EVERY DAY." A bite from one of the larger rattlesnakes is a very serious affair. If such should transpire, promptitude without the loss of the fraction of a second is imperative. Carelessness with the venomous snakes is a positive crime. The reputation and lives of the men in the Reptile House are involved with their handling of the venomous snakes. BE CAUTIOUS."

Ditmars was wrong, but also right. A big belt of whiskey was the traditional method of fighting snakebite, as some old Western films testify. Chugging whiskey spreads venom through the body, since it speeds up blood circulation. As for ligatures, they seem to localize the venom, and in some cases, such as rattlesnake bites, may increase tissue damage. Once the ligature, or torniquet, has been released, venom may flood the body, causing explosive damage. As for sucking out the venom by mouth, that is a bad tactic. Venom may damage the tissues of the mouth and, worse yet, enter cuts or abrasions. However, removing venom, which usually pools below the skin before it spreads, remains a good idea. One way to do it with little or no risk, favored by many authorities on treating snakebite, is to use a mechanical suction device, a small, hand-held pump that

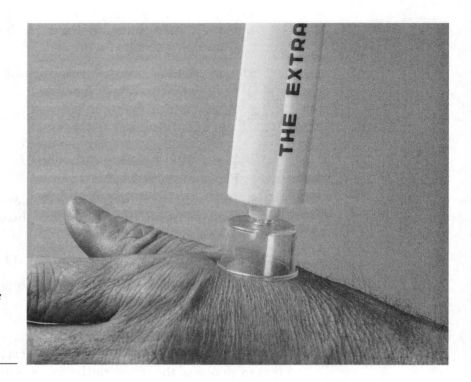

The Sawyer Extractor *is widely used to remove venom from the bites of snakes and other venomous animals.*

extracts venom from the point of fang penetration. The device used most is the *Sawyer Extractor,* which creates a strong vacuum to suction out poisons and other foreign fluids. (It is useful against other venomous bites, including those of bees, wasps and spiders.) I keep a *Sawyer* kit in the first-aid kit that I carry in my vehicle, just in case.

Suction devices such as the *Extractor* are for emergency first aid. Other first-aid measures include washing the bite with soap and water and keeping the site of the bite lower than the heart.

The key, however, is to seek immediate medical help, if possible. Identification of the species inflicting the bite is important, even if the description is tenuous. Usually, a tetanus immunization is called for, as the teeth of snakes—non-venomous as well as venomous—can carry bacteria and other pathogens. Antibiotics, not available in Ditmars' time, are mostly used to combat infection, often a secondary result of snakebite.

The key to saving someone from the bites of highly venomous snakes, however, is antivenin, a product derived from the blood serum of domestic animals, usually horses, that have been periodically injected with low doses of snake venom. The host animal builds up antibodies to the venom, which, when delivered in the serum to bite victims, helps neutralize the poison.

Antivenins were first developed in the late 1800s. For successful treatment, an antivenin must be specific to the chemistry of the venom in the snake that has caused the bite. Antivenin for a cobra may not be helpful treating the bite of a rattlesnake. And there are some snakes (such as the St. Lucia serpent, a pit viper, and the long-glanded coral snake) for which antivenin has not been developed. Beyond that, some people are sensitive to horse serum, just as individuals may be allergic to dog or cat hair, so the administration of antivenin may cause adverse reactions. Even so, antivenin is the best treatment. It saves lives. Many zoos and hospitals maintain a stockpile of antivenins. Typically, major zoos cooperate with police and public health authorities in establishing emergency protocols for speeding antivenins to snake bite victims.

A major source of antivenins for elapids and vipers is the Thai Red Cross Society, which has facilities for keeping venomous snakes and extracting their venom by "milking" their fangs, a procedure best left to experts. During the mid-1970s, I visited the society's "snake farm" and institute in Bangkok. Inside the large building of yellowed stone, with a façade of arches, were walled pits, in which lived king cobras, Russell's vipers and a bevy of other highly venomous snakes. The snakes were kept fat and happy because healthy snakes produce more venom. I could not help but make analogy: the snake farm was quite like a dairy farm, where animals were maintained for the products they produced.

The Nature of Venom

Scientists used to classify snake venoms into three categories, according to their physiological activity: neurotoxins (which attack the nervous system), hemotoxins (which attack the blood system), and cardiotoxins (which attack the heart and associated organs). More recent evidence indicates that venoms are a witch's brew of ingredients and that any toxins they can contain—proteins for the most part—can assault more than one organ system in the body. At the same time, however, the venoms of various snakes overtly display different activities. By and large, for example, viper and pit viper venoms cause substantial tissue damage in and around the bite; inhibition of coagulation, blood vessel injury; and often damage to the heart, kidneys and lungs. Envenomation by most rattlesnakes and many other pit vipers usually causes severe and immediate pain. Swelling erupts around the bite and, if untreated, spreads. The skin and nearby tissue around the bite thickens and becomes glossy, then erupts, discolors, and deteriorates. The victim may feel week and even faint. Nausea and sweating may occur and parts of the body even far from the bite—such as the mouth and scalp—may become numb. Bites from vipers, as opposed to pit vipers, have similar symptoms, except that the clotting mechanism of the blood is vastly inhibited. Blood may pour from the wound, the gums, and internal organs.

Two cases of rattlesnake bites, both in zoos and many years apart, illustrate some of the symptoms of pit viper envenomation. The first to occur, on January 27, 1916, resulted in a medical milestone. Bronx Zoo keeper John Toomey was nailed by a western diamondback rattlesnake as he was cleaning a cage in the reptile house. The enclosure housed several diamondbacks that had recently arrived from Texas. Toomey opened the cage door slightly, then reached in with a long-handled shovel to remove some feces. At the opposite side of the cage lay coiled a large rattler, perhaps 10 pounds in weight. As Toomey prepared to scoop up the waste, the snake launched an explosive strike, shooting across the cage and burying its fangs in the keeper's left arm. The stricken man shook off the snake, slammed the door closed and fell back, calling to his fellow keepers. Quickly, they placed ligatures above and below the wound. The zoo's veterinarian and a physician were summoned. The physician treated Toomey with cobra antivenin from the zoo's stockpile. At that time, the sole serum available in the United States to treat snakebite was for use against the venoms of cobras and their kin. From the manner in which Toomey's condition worsened, it was apparent that the cobra serum would not inhibit the effects of rattlesnake venom.

Toomey's hand and arm swelled mightily. He began to vomit. He was rushed to a hospital, where he sank into a coma as the swelling spread to the entire left side of his upper body.

Physicians were stumped. It appeared that Toomey could very well die. Then it was reported that a physician from Brazil had recently developed a serum effective against the bites of pit vipers. And, astoundingly, he was at that very moment attending a scientific meeting in New York City, carrying along samples of his serum. The Brazilian was called in and his serum administered to Toomey. He showed immediate improvement and was discharged from the hospital three weeks later.

Years later, on November 4, 1959, Gary K. Clarke, an employee of the San Diego Zoo who later became one of the country's most respected zoo directors, was bitten by a red diamond rattlesnake, which inhabits Baja California and the extreme southwest of the State of California. Clarke, an expert snake handler, was 20 years of age at the time, six feet tall and 154 pounds. He recorded the entire sequence of events, leading to the bite and thereafter, in the herpetological journal *Copeia*. It was a remarkable feat because the bulk of his notes were made while he was in extreme pain. Clarke was studying the metabolism of snakes and thus he weighed specimens periodically. His method was to place the snake in a cloth sack that had been draped over the back of a chair and put it on the scales. Normally, Clarke had an assistant with him during the weighing process. However, on this day, the assistant was unavailable so Clarke opted to go it alone.

Clarke grabbed the snake behind the head with his right hand and held the middle of its body with his left. For five minutes, the snake calmly resisted Clarke's efforts to place it in the bag. Clarke released his grip on the snake's body so he could hold the bag open. The snake began to flail, violently, so Clarke had to grasp its body once again. During the struggle, the bag fell to the floor. Clarke, the rattler still in his grip, knelt down and rearranged the sack with his teeth. The snake repeatedly tried to bite. Despite his awkward position—if the term can even be used in such a situation—Clarke managed to slip the snake inside the sack and knot it. Rising to his feet, his right hand just above the knot, Clarke left the sack on the floor about a foot away. As he lifted the bag, the snake went wild inside it. It struck and its fangs went through the sack, through Clarke's trousers and into his left leg just below the knee. For a moment, the snake hung there by its fangs until Clarke shook it loose.

Clarke noticed that venom was sprayed on the floor. Although he had felt a stab of white-hot pain, he figured that the snake had expelled most of its venom outside of the wound. Clarke even thought of continuing his work. He treated himself with a snakebite kit, then called his supervisor for help. Blood seeped from the bite and the zoo man had to sit down. Minutes later he was in an ambulance headed to a hospital.

Clarke meticulously recorded what happened in the ensuing week, after which he was discharged from the hospital. He was extremely weak and, for several hours, could not urinate. He had a slight temperature. His blood pressure was on a roller coaster of ups and downs. He was nauseated. "Feel terrible," he wrote. His entire leg was swollen and its muscles pulsated uncontrollably. His leg was so sensitive to pain that even the breath of a physician treating him and the light of a flash bulb— a photographer was summoned to record the bite—caused tremendous agony. Clarke has said that the pain was almost unendurable. Even morphine had little effect against it. Treated with antivenin and drugs, he slowly recovered. But not before a massive attack of hives spread over most of his body, which almost sealed his eyes.

Ironically, as rattlesnakes go, the species that bit Clarke is extremely placid and not considered highly venomous. Clarke believed that the snake was so disturbed that it emptied the entire contents of its venom glands, so that even if some of the poison ended up on the floor, enough was left to introduce a massive infusion into his leg.

Zoo men who handle snakes on a regular basis have often figured in sensational cases of snakebite. One such involved the best-known zoo figure of the last half-century, at least in the eyes of the public: the late R. Marlin Perkins, director of the St. Louis Zoo and star of the *Mutual of Omaha's Wild Kingdom*, which ran on television for what seemed like eons. The case was reported in the *Bulletin of the Antivenin Institute of America*, July 1929. The account is a dramatic example of what happens when a human is bitten by a viper.

At 9:50 A.M., Perkins, then reptile curator in St. Louis, was treating a Gaboon viper for parasites, with the help of his associate, Moody Lentz, a man who was not widely known to the public but who became highly respected in zoo circles. The snake sank one fang into the upper surface of Perkins' left index finger. Immediately, Perkins felt extreme pain in the finger, fol-

Okinawan habu (Trimeresurus flavoviridis)

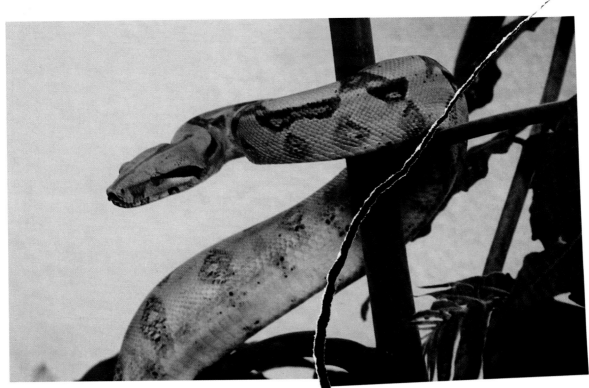

Boa constrictor (Boa constrictor)

Yellow anaconda
(Eunectes noteaus)

Burmese python (Python
molurus biveittatus)

Rock python (Python sebae)

Eastern indigo snake
(Dymarchon corais couperi)

Black racer (juvenile)
(Coluber constrictor
constrictor)

Ringneck snake
(Diadophis punctatus)

WIL MARA

Black pine snake
(Pituophis melanoleucus
lodingi)

LINDA KRULIKOWSKI

Florida pine snake (Pituophis melanoleucus mugitus)

WIL MARA

Great Plains rat snake (Elaphe
guttata emoryi)

WIL MARA

LINDA KRULIKOWSKI

Black rat snake (Elaphe obsoleta obsoleta)

Corn snake (Elaphe
guttata guttata)

LINDA KRULIKOWSKI

Western coachwhip (Masticophis flagellum testaceus)

Northern water snake (Nerodia sipedon)

Eastern garter snake (Thamnophis sirtalis sirtalis)

Rainbow boa (Epicrates cenchria)

Egg-eating snake (Dasypeltis scaber)

Green tree python (Chondropython viridis)

lowed by pain in his hand, which spread into his chest towards his heart. His arm ballooned and his pulse rate dropped to 80. Perkins was rushed to a hospital, where he began lapsing into shock. His pulse dropped to the point at which it could not be detected. Perkins was unconscious and his eyes did not react to light. Blood vessels began to hemorrhage and his arm blackened as tissues broke down. Perkins was near death. With acumen remarkable for the time, the hospital staff saved Perkins, through intensive treatment, involving administration of antivenin, fluids, drugs and blood transfusions. Even so it took months before he was fully recovered.

TONGUE-TIED BY A COPPERHEAD

Not all pit vipers have highly toxic venom. The North American copperhead is one of these. A docile snake which sometimes fails to strike even when stepped upon—easy to do because the copperhead's coloration blends with fallen leaves—the copperhead is regarded as relatively benign. I know several people who have been bitten with results less painful than a wasp bite. Only about a half dozen fatalities from copperhead bites are known. Most were either young children, who received little in the way of treatment, or older adults, at least one of whom had imbibed whisky, which, as previously noted, increases the flow of venom through the blood. The following account puts the venom of the copperhead into perspective.

James Oliver was a superb teller of stories. He had an easy-going sense of humor. On at least one occasion, however, he told a story where the humor verged on black. The point of the incident he related was to dramatize the fact that the venom of the copperhead is relatively mild, compared to those of most other pit vipers. Here it is, from his days as curator of reptiles at the Bronx Zoo:

Oliver was sitting at his desk in the zoo's administration building when the receptionist in the lobby rang his secretary. A stocky young man, probably in his early twenties, highly agitated and disheveled, wanted to see someone in the reptile department. The secretary went to the lobby and returned, flustered herself. She reported that the visitor claimed he had been bitten on the tongue by a copperhead. More than curious, Oliver went to the lobby and asked the young man to describe his problem. Obviously in pain, struggling to speak, the visitor croaked, "Ooi waz itten aye ah cop'had."

Disbelieving, Oliver asked the man to "speak more distinctly." As Oliver related it, "He gesticulated frantically, pointing towards his mouth and trying to speak clearly."

Desperately the man replied, "Ooi waz iteen by ah aake, a cop'had shake." The last word, said Oliver, was a "slowly hissed scream."

Then the visitor stuck out his tongue, which was black, cracked and peeling. Upon ex-amining the tongue, Oliver turned believer and asked the sufferer how and when it happened.

"Inah aar, in Phelphia, lash niht," the man replied.

As it turned out, the snake-bitten visitor was a merchant seaman whose ship had stopped at Philadelphia. Somehow, during an excursion into the surrounding countryside, he had found a very small copperhead and managed to get it in a jar. How the seaman did it, Oliver never told me. Perhaps he did not know. The fact that the young man was able to jar a copperhead without being bitten right then and there testifies to the natural docility of the species. At any rate, the seaman returned to his vessel to show the snake to his shipmates. As seamen in port are wont to do, they all headed to a waterfront saloon, taking the jarred snake with them. Once there, the serpent was promptly dumped on to the bar top. Alarmed, it coiled, flicking its tongue. The young man's friends dared him to stick out his own tongue and touch that of the snake. Bad move. The snake nailed the young seaman's tongue. For some reason, perhaps the reputation for expertise of the Bronx Zoo's reptile de-partment, the copperhead victim boarded a train for New York, and thus arrived at Oliver's door. Oliver assured him that he was not in mortal danger, despite the severe pain and tis-sue destruction caused by the bite. The seaman went to a local hospital and was treated. Emergency room personnel probably had a field day talking about that case.

An incident that happened to me puts this weird case in perspective. I was bitten in-side the lower lip by a wasp. Within minutes, swelling and numbness spread through my mouth and into my throat. I feared that my breathing might be impaired. I, too, went to an emergency room for treatment, which obviously worked. I may have been in more danger from the sting of a wasp than the seafarer was from a copperhead bite.

The tissue damage caused by elapid venoms is less than that from vipers, but these venoms strongly attack sensory and motor functions and also cause cardiac and respiratory prob-lems. Elapids differ so widely that the symptoms of a bite vary greatly. Cobra bites are usually followed by intense pain with 10 minutes or so after the event. However, the swelling that occurs after viper and pit viper strikes is not nearly as evident or wide-spread. After a cobra bite, the victim becomes drowsy and finds it difficult to breathe. The larynx, as well as muscles throughout the body and particularly around the face, may become para-lyzed. Sensory functions, such as vision, become scrambled. In extreme cases, the victim may lapse into coma.

The impact of cobra venom usually occurs within a half hour after the bite. As the following case of cobra bite testifies, the symptoms of cobra bite, while no less dangerous that that of a pit viper, are soporific, rather than horrendously painful. Carl F. Kauffeld, director of the Staten Island Zoo in New York City and a top herpetologist, survived a cobra bite and described his reaction in the *Philadelphia Herpetological Society Bulletin*, 1963. In effect, he became detached from the world. He wrote that he was not unconscious but unaware of his surroundings. Pain was nonexistent; he was not anxious. Gentle darkness closed in upon him. He later wrote that the manner of death from cobra poisoning might be "not at all unpleasant."

Flashback into history. Cleopatra allegedly used an "asp" to commit suicide. The term "asp" is a common name applied to various snakes, including the European viper and the Egyptian cobra. Historians and herpetologists alike suspect that the snake which Cleopatra used to do herself in was an Egyptian cobra. Given the nasty effects of viper bite and the symptoms that Kauffeld described, Cleopatra—obviously no fool—would logically have chosen the cobra as the way out.

Sea snake venom is rather unusual. It is slow-acting but extremely dangerous. Its impact is usually not felt for several hours. After that, the muscles ache viciously and then weaken. The kidneys and heart begin to malfunction. Untreated, the bite of most sea snakes can lead to death within a day or two.

The Evolution and Role of Snake Venom

As evidenced by the fact that venomous snakes do not always inject their poison when striking in defense, venom is believed to be primarily a means of feeding on creatures that, for other predators, would be a tough nut to swallow. (This is not to discount its role as a defensive measure.) The fact that a big anaconda or python can gulp down a pig weighing more than 100 pounds is no more sensational than the ability of a foot-long garter snake, about the diameter of a human pinky, to devour and easily digest a fat toad, long rear limbs and all. By and large, venom—and, as will be discussed, the ability to deliver it—are the properties of the most advanced snakes, those that appeared relatively late in serpent evolution. Some snakes have venom so specialized that it works effectively only against a certain type of prey. There is a serpent that lives in the seaside marshes of Indonesia that eats mainly crabs and its venom acts far more quickly and efficiently on those crustaceans than on other creatures.

The prime predatory advantages of venom are twofold. Venom immobilizes the prey, often by killing it within moments and making it much easier to swallow. But the worth of venom to a snake does not stop there. The enzymes in venom begin to break down the tissues of the victim almost immediately, in effect starting the digestive process. Once the prey is within the snake, the digestive capabilities of venom continue to operate. These chemicals work in tandem with those already present in the snake's digestive system. The prey is subjected to a double dose of digestion, allowing the snake to absorb a heavy meal quite efficiently. (The digestive capabilities of venom are not peculiar to snakes. Spider venom works in a similar way.)

The glands that manufacture venom are present in many snakes that are not considered "venomous." Since the 1960s, evidence has mounted that at least some of these snakes do indeed produce venom, but are not considered dangerous because they do not have the structural and dental apparatus to deliver it. The structure of a particular snake's jaw and the nature of its teeth dictate how efficiently it can introduce venom into prey or enemies. It has become increasingly evident that many snakes classified as non-venomous do have potential for producing some degree of venom, although from an evolutionary standpoint they pose little or no danger to humans. This applies especially to the colubrids, most of which posssess the Durernoy's gland, which has venom-manufacturing potential.

One case of envemonation from a supposedly "non-venomous" colubrid snake, in 1975, sparked the interest of experts in the field. A boy of 11 years, in Camavillo, California, picked up a garter snake, a species that I have handled many times without unpleasant results, other than a release of smelly musk from the anal glands. This youngster spotted the snake in his school yard and picked it up. Garter snakes are rather fiesty; this one was a brawler. It bit the child and fastened its teeth into its flesh so firmly that a school custodian had to pry the serpent's jaws loose with a screw driver. The snake's tiny teeth—which can barely be seen on a live specimen—were locked in so long that, apparently, some sort of toxic substance flowed into the wound. At least, that is what some of the most prominent experts on snake venom of the time, who reviewed the case, believed. While the boy remained in school, his arm, the site of the bite, began to swell. The swelling spread upwards toward the shoulder and the skin blackened. The boy—together with the snake, which had been killed—were flown to the Los Angeles County-University of California Medical Center, where he was successfully treated.

The hognose snake, whose defensive posture mimics that of a viper, may also have venomous potential. Its bluff may not be all bluster. In 1960, a well-known herpetologist, Arthur Bragg, was bitten by a hognose snake in the hand. Pain and swelling lasted for several days. Some years later, a teenager reported a hognose bite that lead to similar symptoms. Some scientists suggest that apparent venom poisoning from hognose snake bites is not really what it seems. These snakes feed mostly on toads, which have skin glands that produce toxins (never rub your eyes with unwashed hands after handling a toad). It may be that these toxins in the snake's mouth that cause the rare occasions of envemonation from hognose snake strikes.

Be that as it may, evidence has mounted that the glands that produce venom may be present in many snakes. How much venom, and how toxic, and how it is delivered, make the difference between whether or not a snake is dangerous or harmless to humans.

IMMUNITY TO VENOM

Snake venom can be a two-edged sword—for snakes. It works against snakes as well as other animals. Cottonmouths have killed rattlesnakes with a venomous bite, sometimes in order to obtain a meal. There are reports describing how snakes of the same species, kept in cages, have killed one another with venomous bites. In fact, an individual snake can kill itself with its own venom. Authenticated accounts tell how rattlers, under duress, have gone wild and bitten themselves, and subsequently died. Scientists are unsure how the venom of a snake affects other venomous snake species or even its own. Many snakes seem to have substantial resistance to venom of conspecifics and even of other related serpents. But it may be a question of tolerance. In the laboratory, massive injections of venom have killed venonous snakes that, under natural circumstances, would be resistant.

There are some givens. The North American king snakes, which regularly eat rattlesnakes, seem immune to pit viper venom, at least in doses administered in rattler bites.

Rattlesnakes usually will not strike a predatory king snake but, instead, try to outmuscle it with coil power.

A few mammals demonstrate resistance, if not immunity, to snakebite. The meerkat, a mongoose-like African animal, has been reported resistant to the venom of cobras, and occasionally feeds on them. Ironically, mongooses themselves, despite their reputation for immunity to cobra venom, seem to have it only in a slight degree. The mongoose uses quickness and agility when it tries to kill and eat snakes. As for humans, some primitive peoples believe that drinking snake venom confers immunity, but this has never been scientifically proven. Over the years, a few herpetologists have tried to immunize themselves against specific snake venoms by undergoing repeated injections of the poison and, in some cases, it seems to have worked.

The Business End

Fangs are the delivery system; the business end of a snake's venom apparatus. The structure and position of venomous fangs are an indication of the snake's position on the serpents' evolutionary tree. Venomous serpents replace old fangs with new ones. The most primitive venomous fangs belong to colubrids. These are rear-fanged snakes, with the delivery mechanism far back in their jaws. Some rear-fanged snakes have fangs that resemble their other teeth, but are longer. These fangs are not very efficient for delivery of venom, which simply drips down the tooth into the bite. This may be the remains of the beginnings of the venom adaptation in snakes. Snakes with fangs of this type feed on creatures such as small birds, small mammals, and lizards. The teeth up front in the jaws secure and damage the prey. On the way down, after considerable chewing on the part of the snake, the fangs in the rear introduce the venom, completing the job. The most dangerous of the rear-fanged colubrids have grooves in their fangs that serve as a venom channel, delivering the venom faster and more directly. Even so, these snakes still must grab a hold and chomp away to bring their poison-bearing teeth into play.

Among the most dangerous of such snakes is the boomslang, a tree snake that averages five feet long, of southern Africa. People who have been bitten by the boomslang on fleshy parts of the body, such as the buttocks—it has happened—generally have suffered few serious effects. The snake usually can not produce a sufficient gape of jaw to bring its fangs into deadly play. But if a boomslang can grab onto a smaller body part, such as a finger, and hold, chewing in its poison, there is serious trouble ahead due to the fact that the boomslang's venom is highly toxic.

Evidence of what a boomslang can do under the right—or, from the victim's perspective, wrong—circumstances is shown by a bite that killed a man who was arguably one of the top herpetologists of the twentieth century, Karl Schmidt. In 1957, when Schmidt was 67 years old, he made a fatal mistake demonstrating that even the best of snake handlers can be bested by the serpents they know so well. Schmidt was working for the Field Museum of Natural History in Chicago when a snake was sent there for identification. A co-worker held the snake behind the neck while Schmidt examined it. It was, in his opinion, a boomslang. While talking to his helper, Schmidt made a fatal mistake. Absent mindedly, he grasped the snake behind the head, an appropriate procedure if the hand is placed directly behind the skull. Schmidt, however, placed his hand a mite further down the snake's body. With a lightning twist, the snake embedded one fang in the herpetologist's thumb.

As the wound bled profusely, Schmidt tried to extract the venom by suction. The snake was a young specimen and because of that and the fact that only one fang had penetrated, Schmidt was not terribly worried. He assumed that only a small amount of venom had entered the wound. He did not feel concern even when he experienced nausea on the train ride home after work. That night, he vomited and his gums began to bleed, but in the morning, he felt much better and even telephoned the museum to say that he would return to work the next day.

He was overly optimistic. As the morning passed, he began to vomit again. His breathing became labored. His wife called for medical help and Schmidt was rushed to the hospital. By 3:00 P.M., he was dead.

Cobras and other elapids, as well as sea snakes, have fangs in the typical up-front position. Their fangs, due to the position and the presence in most of an enclosed groove to channel venom, represent an evolutionary step forward from the rear-fanged snakes. Elapids have relatively short fangs. Those of an adult Indian cobra are about five millimeters long; a green mamba's can be a couple of millimeters longer than that; the coral snakes of North America have two-millimeter fangs. The short fangs of cobras and their relatives sometimes have difficulty penetrating thick clothing or animal hides. These snakes sometimes must strike more than once to score a direct hit.

SPITTING COBRAS

A handful of cobras, including the ringhals, which has an open venom groove, and spitting cobra, both of Africa, have the ability to squirt venom from the openings in their fangs for a distance of six to nine feet. They are able to do so because the muscles around their venom glands are extra strong. These super-specialized snakes aim for the eyes, with remarkable accuracy. If not washed out, venom that enters the eyes can cause blindness, not to mention serious pain. The venom of the ringhals is particularly toxic. It can damage even unbroken skin.

It is the vipers and pit vipers whose fangs reach the evolutionary zenith. Some of the vipers and pit vipers have the longest fangs of any snakes. Those of the Gaboon viper, the species that bit Marlin Perkins, are almost two inches long. Some of the largest rattlesnakes have fangs approaching an inch. Generally, by the way, the bigger and older the snake, the more impressive its fangs relative to species—since growth in snakes is continuous.

The fangs of vipers and pit vipers are a marvel of evolutionary engineering. Sharp as a hypodermic needle, they curve inward, allowing them to embed deeply when striking. A tube for conducting venom, rather than a groove, runs along the interior of the fang, and exits through vertical slots on the front of the tooth. This apparatus literally injects venom. The tips of the fangs are edged bevel-fashion, so the snake needs only to jab rather than bite. At rest, the fangs lie against the snake's upper jaw, out of harm's way. When the snake strikes, the upper jaw swivels upwards and forwards, so that they stab almost horizontally. The fangs of a large viper or pit viper can be incredibly strong. I know of one instance in which the tire of a pickup truck was flattened when it ran over a large eastern diamondback, and the snake responded with a strike. On the other hand, some small species of rattlers have fangs that are considerably less effective. In the Florida Everglades, a pygmy rattlesnake only about a foot long, hit my leather boot twice, and never even made a mark.

How Fast a Strike?

The speed at which venomous snakes strike has been somewhat overrated, although it still is impressive. In order to strike at the proper angle, a cobra must rear up the front of its body. Then it strikes downward. Even then, it lacks blinding speed. Experienced—very experienced—snake handlers have been known to grab a cobra behind the head as it launches its attack.

Rattlesnakes are much faster but, again, not as quick as many people believe. In the 1950s, a scientist conducted an unusual experiment to determine the speed of a rattlesnake's strike. Dr. Walker Van Riper of the Denver Museum of Natural History used strobes and what was then high-speed photography to time the strike of a rattlesnake. He found that its head moved at about eight feet per second. As a former boxer with a decent left jab, I have always been intrigued by Riper's experiment. He timed his own, inexperienced left jab at 18.1 feet per second. He estimated that the jab of a skilled boxer could travel faster than the head of a striking rattlesnake. Having been tattooed by the jabs of certain opponents in my youth, I think that Van Riper was correct.

CHAPTER 8

Snakebite Around the Globe

Although accurate figures are hard to come by, it is generally accepted in herpetological circles that worldwide, about 300,000 people are bitten by snakes each year. Obviously, this is a rough figure, since many cases in undeveloped counties of the tropics and subtropics, where most bites occur, undoubtedly go unreported.

Snakebite in the United States

It is estimated that about 8,000 people are bitten by venomous snakes annually in the United States. Of this number only about a dozen cases are fatal, far less than the deaths due to reactions to the stings of bees and wasps. About a third of bite victims are zoo personnel who have regular contact with snakes, or people who keep venomous snakes in their homes. Almost all of the bites in the wild are from rattlesnakes; more than a dozen species inhabit the United States and, of these, the eastern and western diamondbacks are especially dangerous, due to their large size and fangs when adult, and the toxicity of their venom.

Alaska, Hawaii, northern New England, and the upper Midwest are free from venomous snakes. The southeastern and southwestern parts of the country, however, are home to the largest numbers and varieties of venomous serpents in the land; not surprisingly, these areas have the highest rates of snake bites.

Snakebite in Europe

Outside of Antarctica, which has no land animals, Europe, separated politically if not geologically from Asia, is the continent on which one is least likely to be bitten by a venomous snake. The chances of being hit by a venomous snake in Europe are infinitely less than being bashed by a Volkswagen. Exact numbers are not available but the number of people bitten annually on the entire continent is significantly less than in the United States alone, and deaths are even less common. One reason is that so much of Europe, especially northern areas, is inhospitable to snakes, venomous or not (see Chapter 4). The other is that snakes, along with wolves, bears and other animals deemed hostile to humans, have dwindled due to the activities of our species. There are only a dozen venomous snakes in Europe. Of these, only a few are truly dangerous and these snakes are by and large species whose ranges extend into Europe from the Middle East. Most venomous is the sand viper, native to central and eastern Europe and through the Middle East. Although its name implies that it is a desert snake, it is not, at least not exclusively. It likes dry, sandy habitat, but prefers to live in rocky areas, especially on sunny slopes where it lies within stony niches, such as the crevice in a riverside cliff in Croatia where I once found three sand vipers snuggled up and basking. The viper often coils and scrunches down in sandy soil, its grayish color camouflaging it extremely well. The other European species with dangerously toxic venom are the blunt-nosed viper, which can be found in the Caucasus, and the coastal viper, present in a tiny area of European Turkey. If one counts the northern fringes of the Caspian Sea region as Europe, then the Asiatic pit viper may be included among truly dangerous European snakes.

The most widespread of European snakes, the adder (a viper) has venom of moderate toxicity. It is the sole venomous serpent native to Britain. Several thousand people are bitten by the adder annually in Europe but during the last century only about a 100 of these cases have been fatal. Often, in fact, adder victims do not even require hospitalization.

Snakebite in Australia

About half of the 130 species of snakes in Australia are venomous and more than a dozen, such as the tiger snake and taipan, are extremely dangerous. Both of these species can be savagely aggressive. The taipan, which has half-inch fangs that have been known to penetrate shoe and sock, carries enough venom to kill several adults. Taipans are so swift that they sometime strike several times before the victim has time to react. It has been known to attack people without provocation— or, at least provocation as we humans understand it. In one well-documented case, a woman was fatally bitten by a taipan while she was walking home from a movie. In the scientific literature, the taipan is repeatedly referred to as one of the most potentially lethal snakes on Earth.

The venom of the tiger snake is even more powerful than that of the taipan. Unlike the taipan, it is not known for random attacks, nor is it as agile. However, if it feels in danger and cannot retreat, it counter attacks viciously. Another of Australia's serpentine terrors is the aptly named death adder. (It is an elapid, not an adder, but earned its name because it resembles vipers in form and behavior.) It is active mainly at night. During the day it conceals itself in dry soil. If disturbed in its hiding place, the death adder does like to give ground, but will defend itself. Its toxin is not quite as powerful as those of the taipan and tiger snake, but it is sufficiently powerful to cause a 50 percent fatality rate if a bite is untreated.

It might seem that one might have to walk on tiptoes to escape dangerous snakes in Australia. That is far from the case. Proportionally, in terms of population, Australia has approximately the same number of snakebites, and snakebite fatalities, as the United States. Luckily for Australians, the most dangerous snakes there either have relatively limited ranges and/or live in habitats that humans shun—except for many Aboriginal Australians, who are much more familiar with the continent's snake fauna than their fellow citizens who have been transplanted from abroad.

The death adder has a sizeable range, here and there across Australia, but usually remains in dry scrub areas where there is little contact with humans. The tiger snake is restricted to southern Australia and Tasmania, but has a very specific habitat, areas that are wet, brushy and rocky. Human intrusion on such areas is minimal. The taipan has a range that is even more restricted. It inhabits scattered, isolated areas of northeastern Australia. It also is extremely rare. The first specimen of taipan known to science was killed in 1867 in Queensland. It was more than a half century later until another specimen was reported.

The most bites and most fatal cases from Australian snakes are not from the most venomous and aggressive of the continent's serpents, but from a second stringer, as far as toxicity and venom are concerned. It is the Australian brown snake. If the power of snake venom were likened to that of gasoline at the pump, that of the brown snake would be medium, but not premium, grade; not the most potent, but enough to get the job done. The toll taken by the brown snake results not only because its venom is relatively toxic but because it is widespread and common, even in grain-growing areas, where it can come into contact with agricultural workers.

Snakebite in Africa

Africa is the home of many species of venomous snakes, including colubrids, elapids and vipers. A significant number of African snakes are considered extremely dangerous and many of them are extremely common. However, as far as the records are concerned, snakebite is not as serious a public health problem in Africa as it is in tropical Asia and Latin America. There are few if any reliable reporting systems when it comes to snakebite in Africa but, by most estimates, 1,000 people die there a year from this cause. The number is really an assumption, so it could vary greatly. African colubrids include the boomslang and an equally dangerous relative, the bird snake. Cobras, which evolved in Africa, reach their greatest diversity there. The Egyptian cobra, found in the northern three-quarters of the continent, except for rain forest, is responsible for a large number of bites, partly because it lives in areas, such as the Nile Valley, with highly concentrated human populations. The Egyptian cobra often lives close to large cities and has been collected in the fast-spreading outskirts of Nairobi, Kenya.

As far as toxicity of venom is concerned, the deadliest snake in Africa is the black mamba, which lives from Ethiopia to South Africa, mostly in bush country. Up to 14 feet long, but no thicker than the butt of a pool cue, the black mamba, a terrestrial species, is believed to be the fastest of all snakes. It is said to be capable of traveling over the ground at seven miles an hour. Given its quickness, the black mamba strikes like lightning. Its bite is so toxic that it is usually fatal, sometimes within minutes, even if antivenin is administered. However, the black mamba is not particularly aggressive and will usually flee from human disturbance if it has the chance, so its bites are infrequent. Three species of so-called "green mambas" also inhabit Africa. Arboreal in habit, they are dangerous, but not nearly so much as their black cousin.

The snake believed responsible for the most bites in Africa is a viper, the puff adder, thick-bodied and sluggish, widespread and common on grasslands and in bush south of the Sahara. The puff adder is qualified as a man-killer for several reasons. It has strong venom, although not as powerful as the black mamba's. It has the typically efficient venom-delivery systems of the vipers. It often lives within areas of high human population. And it hunkers down, hidden when approached, so is often unencountered by unwary walkers.

Snakebite in Asia

The preponderance of the world's snakebites occur in southern Asia. In this part of the world, vast numbers of people, many of whom go barefoot, live close to a wide array of venomous snakes. The numbers of both snakes and people in the region make unpleasant encounters between them common. Many venomous Asian snakes, moreover, feel quite at home amidst humans—in rice paddies where frogs abound, for example, and even in dwellings, where they search for rats. Fatalities from snakebite in southern Asia are estimated as high as 25,000 a year. Perhaps the snake that kills more people than any other is the Asiatic cobra, which is extremely abundant. Its bite can be treated with antivenin, but often victims do not receive medical attention. The king cobra, which has a notorious reputation, is nevertheless implicated in few bites. It is not common, and usually inhabits more remote areas than some of the other Asian cobras. It is also a rather docile snake and tends to flee the approach of people. There are many stories to the contrary, telling of king cobras chasing people, seemingly intent on killing them. These incidents, most herpetologists believe, involve female king cobras defending their nests; they are very attentive mothers.

Kraits, cobra relatives, are also known to be responsible for many deaths in Asia. They are stocky snakes, quiet and docile rather than aggressive. Why are they rated high among Asian serpents as a cause of human death? Their venom is quite toxic. A few milligrams of venom from the Indian krait can kill a human who goes untreated. The venom is so virulent that even when victims receive antivenin, the chances of survival are only 50 percent. Kraits come into contact with people mostly in the night when they are most active. They often roam through the streets of small villages after dark, even creeping into homes. Unlike cobras, which make a great show before striking, rearing up and spreading their hoods, kraits react to the approach of a human in the manner of an African puff adder. They hunker down, which makes an unwary pedestrian on a village path more likely to tread upon them.

Unlike the krait, or even the Asian cobra, the Russell's viper is a feisty snake, which when threatened employs a vigorous defense. Its venom is not as toxic as that of the krait, but when disturbed, it stands its ground and mounts a vigorous defense. This viper is a leading cause of snakebite fatalities in southern Asia.

Snakebite in Central and South America

South America and Central America have rivaled Asia in the number of snakebites and, as well, deaths from envenomation. The snakes of this region that do the most damage are mainly pit vipers, such as the *terciopelo* or *Barba Amarilla*. It is a large pit viper, which is often found in agricultural areas, and thus comes often into contact with people. It is widespread throughout the region and believed to be responsible for more fatalities than any other snake there.

The most dangerous snake in Latin America, ranging from Mexico to the South American tropics, is the neotropical rattlesnake. It is allegedly the most venomous of all pit vipers. Worse yet, it often does not coil and rattle as other rattlers do. It simply strikes without warning. In some areas, it is known as the *breakneck snake* because victims caught in spasms created by the venom often snap their heads backwards.

The tropical American snake with the worst reputation is the bushmaster, the largest pit viper, reaching a length of a dozen feet, and thick of body. It has long fangs and venom at least as toxic as that of the North American diamondbacks. Despite its bad reputation, however, it has not been implicated in many fatalities or even bites. The bushmaster is a creature of the deep forests and dislikes the encroachment of people, so it encounters our species less than many other serpents. Some victims of this snake may have died because they were bitten too far into the jungle to receive medical help. Be that as it may, a relative of mine who was a physician in the American tropics gave me a piece of advice as I was heading into bushmaster country. "If a bushmaster bites you, lie down under a tree and relax, because in a few minutes you will be dead."

The Reality of Snakebite

Venomous snakes do not look for people to bite. They fear—if a serpent can fear—people. The problem arises when venomous snakes and people bump into one another inadvertently, or when people, such as zoo keepers, consciously deal with these deadly reptiles. As people proliferate and move into snake country, the conflict between human and reptile may increase. It has happened in Florida and near my home in Connecticut, where subdivisions have been erected on prime rattlesnake habitat. With their hunting grounds and dens disrupted, the snakes had nowhere to go but to prowl about backyards, frightening the wits, rightfully so, out of home owners. Is there room for venomous snakes in a world of ever-expanding human population? Is there room for grizzly bears? Bears, at least, are furry and sometimes on two legs. Snakes slither on their bellies and are not at all cuddly. No sane person wants to be ripped up by a grizzly or killed by a snake. But what would our world be without them?

CHAPTER 9

Snake Sketches

A book describing each and every species of snake would be a massive volume—or, more likely, volumes—indeed. Here, I provide accounts of species according to their presumed significance to readers. The reasons for selection are varied. Some of these snakes may be frequently seen by people, such as birders, hunters, anglers, and hikers, who spend significant time outdoors. Others are listed because they are highly representative of their family, i.e. the boa constrictor as a member of the family Boidae, or because they have a special fascination for people, as does the king cobra. Others, such as the Java wart snake, are presented because they are oddities. The groupings, i.e. Venomous Snakes, are designed for easy reference and in conjunction with particular chapters in this book. Snakes are arranged according to families and under geographical sub-headings. To find the forest cobra, for example, go to *Venomous Snakes* and then *Africa*. In some cases, a species may span more than one geographical area. For example, the bushmaster ranges from Central America to the Amazon Basin. It is described in the section on South America and the West Indies because it is most commonly associated with South American jungles.

Snakes are listed with their generally accepted common names—"cottonmouth," for example, rather than "water moccasin," which has fallen out of regular usage. In some cases, local or alternative common names are given. The scientific names of each species, in Latin and consisting of two words, are also listed. The first word describes the genus of the snake. A genus, in taxonomical tech talk, is a group of animals or plants whose members are closely related but usually (stress "usually") do not interbreed, as do members of a species. The second name is that of the species. By way of example, the scientific name of the timber rattlesnake is *Crotalus horridus.* The generic name is a Latin derivative of the Greek word, "krotalon," meaning "rattle." The species name, *horridus,* comes from a Latin term meaning that one's hair stands on end, as in fear. Given that the timber rattlesnake, while dangerous, is not particularly aggressive, the name might be a bit off base, but it is engraved in the scientific literature.

Representative Venomous Snakes

This section contains descriptions of some typical and important venomous snakes of the world. Snakes are grouped by geographical regions.

North America
FAMILY: ELAPIDAE
Arizona coral snake (*Micruroides euryxanthus*)

This coral snake, like its king cobra relative, feeds largely on other serpents, usually worm-like blind snakes and other small species. The Arizona coral snake must prey on tiny snakes, because it is small as well, less than two feet long. This snake, which has a very limited range, is primarily a desert and semi-desert species. It is secretive, seeking out rocky areas and dry washes where it can hide from predators. It is found up to a mile high in the mountains. Days are spent hiding in nooks and crannies. At night, the Arizona coral snake hunts, especially if the ground is dampened by rain or heavy dew. Like other coral snakes, it is brightly colored, its body ringed by red and black, between bands of either white or yellow. Despite its small size, this creature is highly venomous.

Range: Southern Arizona and New Mexico into northern Mexico.

Size: About a foot-and-a-half maximum, usually smaller.

Danger Rating: Powerful neurotoxic venom, with potentially fatal consequences. Not aggressive, so bites on humans are mostly accidental. If you see a brightly ringed snake coil up, hide its head in its coils and invert its tail, stay clear.

Remarks: This species, as well as other coral snakes, are secretive, non-aggressive, and come into contact with humans usually by accident. In coral snakes, red rings are separated from black rings by yellow or white. A black head is another trademark of the Arizona coral snake.

Eastern coral snake (*Micrurus fulvius*)

This species is much more widespread than the Arizona coral snake. It lives in several habitats, including grasslands, dry open woods, and fringes of streams and ponds. It may also be found on rocky hillsides. The eastern coral snake is a secretive creature that hides under fallen logs and leaves. Similar in appearance to the Arizona coral snake but it is larger, and only its snout, rather than its entire head, is black. Like most other coral snakes, it feeds on other reptiles, mostly small snakes and lizards.

Range: North Carolina to West Texas, also northeastern Mexico.

Size: Usually about two feet, sometimes larger.

Danger Rating: Very potent venom, but apparently a poor delivery apparatus. Many bites are ineffective. Other times, only small amounts of venom introduced. Nevertheless, this is a very dangerous snake.

Remarks: Most active from early to mid morning. Not aggressive but often tries to bite if restrained. Several different species of coral snakes are scattered around the globe. The eastern coral snake is part of a complex of about 40 species in the genus *Micurus*, which range from the southern United States to Argentina. Other representative species of this genus will be given in subsequent sections of this chapter.

FAMILY: VIPERIDAE
Copperhead (*Agkistrodon contortrix*)

The copperhead is the most abundant and widespread venomous snake in the eastern half of the United States. In many areas, it is the only venomous serpent. Because of its large range, and due to the fact that it is not as adverse to human activities as some other venomous snakes, it is implicated in many snakebite cases. More often than not, a bite results from a human blundering into the snake—when working on a woodpile, for example. These snakes often hide in stone walls, brush piles and debris, such as heaps of discarded boards. It sometimes is abundant in populated areas, such as housing developments that have encroached upon its habitat. Steve Berube, illustrator of this book, is an authority on copperheads in Connecticut. He has convinced homeowners who have these snakes on their property not to dispatch them. Copperheads are quite docile and have been known to crawl over a person's foot without untoward incident. The copperhead has a stout body, patterned with markings that enable it to blend into the leaves of the forest floor. The markings are dark brown to russet, over a body color that ranges from buff pink to orange brown. This snake's name comes from the fact that the top of its head is yellowish to coppery red.

In the spring, when they emerge from their winter dens, usually in rock ledges, copperheads are mainly diurnal because they require sunlight for warmth. A study by Howard K. Reinert of Lehigh University suggests that gravid females prefer warmer temperatures than males, and so tend to congregate on sunnier slopes. As summer warms the air temperatures, copperheads start working the night shift, enabling them to avoid excessive heat but still keep comfortably warm.

Copperheads tend to live in wooded areas, especially where there are rocky hillsides and cliffs. They like dry woods but, even so, if this type of habitat is near streams and ponds, they prefer it even more. Copperheads feed mostly on small mammals and will not turn down nestling ground birds.

Range: Massachusetts to Kansas, south to Texas and the Gulf states, but not in peninsular Florida.

Size: Average to about a yard long, a few up to four feet.

Danger Rating: Bites are painful, but seldom if ever fatal. Several people have told me that the pain that they felt from a copperhead bite is no worse than that of a wasp sting.

Remarks: Copperheads are so well camouflaged on the woodland that people often walk right by them without knowing it. Unlike most of its American pit viper relatives, copperheads often do not become agitated when inadvertently disturbed. They may simply hunker down and wait for the disturbance to pass.

Cottonmouth (*Agkistrodon piscivorus*)

A skunk's black-and-white colors are an example of what scientists call "warning coloration." It serves notice upon potential aggressors to stay away, or risk unpleasant consequences. When an agitated cottonmouth rears back and opens its jaws, the white interior of its mouth is unmistakable. It, too, is a warning, and the consequences of disregarding it can be far more serious that a dousing with skunk spray. The cottonmouth, also called the water moccasin, is a snake to avoid. Its venom packs a wallop, and it can be extremely aggressive and often does not follow the tenet that discretion is the better part of valor. If disturbed, the cottonmouth may well hold its ground and prepare to give battle; it may even take the offensive, going after what it perceives as danger, which may be a hunter, angler, or hiker who has ventured on to its turf.

Cottonmouths have different dietary preferences than most other American pit vipers. They feed mostly on cold-blooded prey, except for occasional birds. Fish, amphibians and other snakes are staples. Given its diet, the cottonmouth is highly aquatic. It is found most often in standing water, such as that of swamps and marshes, shallow lakes and ponds, and warm, slow-moving rivers. Research, including that by Archie Carr, a scientist with whom I traveled through East Africa several years ago, shows that cottonmouths congregate under rookeries of herons and egrets, where they gorge on fish dropped by adult birds feeding their nestlings, and on the nestlings should they fall from the nest.

Range: Primarily the southeastern United States, from southern Virginia through Florida, west to Texas and north to southern Illinois.

Size: Heavy-bodied and large, often three or four feet long but sometimes up to six feet.

Danger Rating: Although bites can be fatal, they usually are not if promptly treated. Even so, tissue damage can be extensive.

Eastern Diamondback Rattlesnake (*Crotalus adamanteus*)

The eastern diamondback rattlesnake is the largest, most venomous snake in the United States and, by most scientific assessments, one of the world's most dangerous snakes. Massive, with inch-long fangs and a venom that attacks the blood, along with other systems in the body, the eastern diamondback is not as aggressive as the cottonmouth, but because of size, potency of its venom and the means to introduce it, this snake can be as deadly as any on the globe.

The eastern diamondback, which derives its name from the olive-green to brown diamond-shaped markings on its back, stalks mammalian prey, ranging in size from mice to cottontail rabbits. It is a lowlander, found only below about 500 feet altitude on the southern Atlantic and Gulf coastal plains. It is most common in sandy, dry pine woods, scrub of pine and turkey oak and palmetto thickets. The eastern diamondback is an excellent swimmer and finds its way to islands in brackish water.

Range: Southeastern North Carolina through Florida, including the keys, to eastern Louisiana.

Size: Three feet to about eight feet.

Danger Rating: Extreme, due to large size, long fangs and highly toxic venom.

Remarks: Development has greatly reduced eastern diamondback numbers. Seldom strays more than 100 miles from the coast. Slightly smaller but almost as dangerous as the eastern diamondback is the western diamondback (*C. atrox*). It ranges from Arkansas to southeastern California and into Mexico.

Sidewinder (*Crotalus cerastes*)

Due to the derogatory use of its name in Western films, the sidewinder is perhaps the most publicized rattlesnake of all.

The name conjures up a sneaky devil, a creature bent on harm. The image is false. The sidewinder is not particularly aggressive and is small, compared to diamondbacks and many other rattlesnakes. It is a retiring sort, which rests during the day partly buried in the sand of the deserts that are its habitat. Most commonly, it is found on sandy flats and dunes where vegetation is sparse. Its scales are keeled, which helps it gain purchase in the sand for its swift lateral motion, from which its name is derived. Throwing its body into loops that literally carry it sideways, it leaves J-shaped markings in its track. Sidewinders hunt for small rodents and lizards mostly after dark, when the desert heat diminishes. The best way to identify a sidewinder is by the presence of a raised, horn-like scale above each eye, which gives it a distinctly evil look.

Range: Southeastern California, southern Nevada, western Arizona and northern Mexico.

Size: About two feet at most.

Danger Rating: Bites can be fatal, but seldom are so.

Remarks: Several other desert vipers, such as sand vipers of Eurasia, use the sidewinding motion for travel.

Timber rattlesnake (*Crotalus horridus*)

The world's "rattlesnake belt" is the southwestern corner of the United States. Like the sidewinder, rattlesnakes thrive in warm, arid conditions. However, a few rattlesnakes have forsaken the ways of their kin. They have opted for habitat far different from parched deserts, sun-baked plains and sandy pine woods. They have sought out the damp, humus-covered ground of cool deciduous forests, where they are, in many cases, the only rattlers around. The most prominent of these is the timber rattlesnake. It is the most widespread rattlesnake in the eastern United States and, in many areas, the only rattlesnake.

Timber rattlesnakes were once very abundant within their range. There are myriad places with names such as "rattlesnake ledges" or "rattlesnake brook," in New England and other parts of the Northeastern United States, which no longer support timber rattlesnake populations.

The timber rattlesnake is generally an upland species, except for the southeastern coastal region, where it haunts canebrakes and is often called the "canebrake rattlesnake." Its dens are usually on rocky, wooded hillsides, especially those with steep ledges and rock slides, where ledges have broken off and piled up down below. Michael W. Klemens, a herpetologist with the American Museum of Natural History in New York City, surveyed den sites and associated foraging areas in Connecticut and found that they are usually above 500 feet. Dens in the portion of the state with the highest altitude, Litchfield County, were usually above 1,000 feet. In parts of its range where there are substantial mountains, such as the southern Appalachians, this species may be found at or even above 6,000 feet. Most timber rattlesnakes forage within a short distance, up to about 2,000 yards, of their dens but some go much farther in search of food, about a mile or two. Preferred prey are rodents, such as chipmunks, and birds.

Range: Southern Maine, New Hampshire and Vermont to northern Florida, south to northern Florida, west to Minnesota and east Texas. Absent from prairie areas.

Size: Average length three to four feet, some to six feet.

Danger Rating: Moderate. Venom is toxic enough to cause fatalities, but this species is mild mannered and seldom strikes before considerable rattling and feints.

Remarks: There are two color phases of this snake, which is characterized by dark black bands on its body. One phase has a yellow background color, making the bands highly visible. The other has a dark background color, which sometimes blends so closely with the bands that the snakes appear almost black.

Pigmy rattlesnake (*Sistrurus miliarius*)

This small rattlesnake lives in habitat similar to that of the eastern diamondback, including Everglades prairie, palmetto scrub, and pinewoods. It has a tiny rattle, with a buzz that can be heard only a yard or so away. There have been an increasing number of encounters between humans and pigmy rattlesnakes as housing developments have spread into snake country.

Range: North Carolina through Florida and west to Texas.

Size: Many adults less than a foot-and-a-half long. A few to about 30 inches.

Danger Rating: There are no known fatalities from the bite of this snake. However, it can be quite painful and produce considerable swelling.

Remarks: A similar species is found in Mexico.

Mexico and Central America

FAMILY: ELAPIDAE
Atlantic coral snake (*Micurus diastema*)

This coral snake is identified by the fact that its black rings are quite narrow, and sometimes number up to 60. Otherwise, it has the typical coral snake coloration, rings of black that alternate with those of yellow and red. The red rings are often dotted with black.

Range: Eastern Mexico to the Honduras, including the Yucatan.

Size: Two to three feet.

Danger Rating: Like other American coral snakes, it has highly toxic venom but not aggressive.

Remarks: American coral snakes in the tropics look so similar that it takes considerable expertise to identify them from a safe distance.

FAMILY: VIPERIDAE
Cantil (*Agkistrodon bilineatus*)

This relative of the copperhead and cottonmouth is a relatively common snake within its range. Like the cottonmouth, it is aquatic and found in wet areas, chiefly in swamps and along streams. It lives largely on fish, amphibians, and birds. The cantil is a dark snake, ranging in color from chocolate-brown to black.

Range: Sonora, Mexico, south to west coast of Guatemala and east coast of Nicaragua.

Size: Two-and-a-half to three feet, rarely more than four feet.

Danger Rating: A dangerous snake whose bite causes severe lesions but seldom is implicated in fatalities.

Remarks: The only snake in its range with a brown coloration and two light stripes on each side of its head.

Barba amarilla (*Bothrops atrox*)

The Barba amarilla's natural habitat is undisturbed forest, where it is often found near streams. However, it has adapted to living in agricultural areas as well. It is the bane of agricultural workers in coffee, cocoa and banana plantations, where it is very common. According to *Poisonous Snakes of the World*, a manual published for U.S. Navy and Marine personnel in 1962, and still an important reference work, the barba amarilla "is probably responsible for more deaths in the Americas than any other snake." Part of the reason for this is that, due to its presence in agricultural areas, the barba amarilla frequently comes into contact with people.

This snake has an unmistakable color pattern. Its background color can be olive-green, gray or brown. Overlying the ground color are pairs of dark triangles, one on each side of the body, edged with black and meeting at their apices at the backbone. The pattern superficially resembles that of the eastern and western diamondback rattlesnakes.

Range: From southern Sonora and southern Tamaulipas in Mexico to Peru and northern Brazil.

Size: A large snake, sometimes reaching eight feet in length.

Danger Rating: High. Long fangs, large size and a very toxic venom make this species exceedingly dangerous.

Remarks: The barba amarilla would rather avoid conflict but if disturbed, counterattacks with repeated strikes. This species is often called the fer-de-lance, an incorrect name. The true fer-de-lance lives only on the island of Martinique.

Lansberg's hognose viper (*Bothrops lansbergii*)

Several small vipers with upturned snouts inhabit drier parts of Mexico, Central America and northern South America. This species is typical of them. It is brown, with paired angular blotches along its body. It seeks out semiarid forest and brush, where it hunts small mammals and ground birds.

Range: Southern Mexico to northern South America.

Size: 18 inches to two feet.

Danger Rating: Not known as a highly dangerous snake, it still is to be avoided.

Remarks: Like other heavy bodied ground vipers, it hunkers down so is not easily seen.

Jumping viper (*Bothrops nummifer*)

This species gets its name from its ability to strike for a longer distance than its body length. It has a brownish body with diamond-shaped markings. The preferred habitat of this snake is in hilly but low rain forests.

Range: Southern Mexico to Panama.

Size: 18 inches to two feet. It has a chunky body.

Danger Rating: Low. Short fangs and venom of low toxicity.

Remarks: Sometimes found in agricultural plantations.

Mexican west-coast rattlesnake (*Crotalus basiliscus*)

This is another rattlesnake with diamond-shaped back markings. It can be confused with a diamondback, but it is the only rattlesnake within its range carrying such markings. It is largely a species of coastal thorn scrub, but also can be encountered on the lower slopes of mountain rain forest.

Range: Western Mexico, from southern Sonora to central Oaxaca.

Size: Usually four or five feet, sometimes a foot or so larger.

Danger Rating: Probably high. There are few scientific accounts about the bite of this snake, but it does produce large amounts of venom that is highly toxic.

Remarks: The prevalence of diamond-shaped markings on so many rattlesnakes suggests that many species radiated from common ancestors with a similar color pattern.

South America and the West Indies

FAMILY: ELAPIDAE

Amazonian coral snake (*Micrurus spixii*)

Coral snakes, although retiring and relatively small, are a highly successful species, evidence of which is that there are 40 species in the New World. That is about twice the number of rattlesnake species. About a half dozen species can be found in South America. Among them is a candidate for the largest of coral snakes, the Amazonian. It has the typical coral snake pattern, bands of red, yellow, and black. It is mainly a species of tropical forests.

Range: The Amazon region.

Size: Usually three to four feet, but sometimes larger, big for a coral snake.

Danger Rating: High. Many fatalities have been attributed to this snake.

Remarks: A close relative, which inhabits the outer margins of the Amazon forest, is the Surinam coral snake (*Micrurus surinamensis*). Competition between the two species is probably low because the Surinam snake, unlike other coral snakes, is semi-aquatic, often eating fish.

FAMILY: VIPERIDAE
Urutu (*Bothrops alternatus*)

Brown, with rounded blotches edged with yellow on its sides, this viper causes a substantial number of bites each year. The urutu lives mainly along streams. It is one of a group of vipers called "lance headed," because their heads are broad, flattened and distinct from the neck. Most of the South American vipers, including those that follow, feed largely on small mammals and birds.

Range: Southern Brazil, Uruguay, Paraguay and northern Argentina.

Size: Usually three to four feet, occasionally five feet.

Danger Rating: Moderate to high. The bite is seldom fatal but causes serious local tissue damage.

Remarks: This snake is one of more than 40 species of lance-headed vipers, actually pit vipers, in tropical America, including most of those that are mentioned here.

Amazonian tree viper (*Bothrops bilineatus*)

Like many tree snakes, this viper has a prehensile tail and is bright green in color. It is a very attractive snake, with a reddish tail tip and a pair of narrow yellow stripes, one on each side of its backbone. It is abundant and has one of the largest ranges of any tree viper in South America.

Range: Amazonia: Brazil, Colombia, Bolivia, Peru, Ecuador, and Venezuela.

Size: About two feet.

Danger Rating: Low. Bite is not particularly damaging.

Remarks: Feeds mostly on birds.

St. Lucia serpent (*Bothrops caribbaeus*)

Few islands of the West Indies are home to venomous snakes. But the snakes that live on those few are highly dangerous. One of them is this species, which inhabits the rugged, hilly rain forest of the island after which it was named. This pit viper also invades agricultural plantations. Its color is pale gray to yellow-gray, with blotches on the sides of its body. It is closely related to the barba amarilla, mentioned earlier, the jararaca (below) and the fer-de-lance (below).

Range: The island of St. Lucia.

Size: Usually three to four feet, sometimes up to seven feet.

Danger Rating: High. Bites cause extreme tissue damage and are often fatal.

Remarks: The close relationship between many members of the genus *Bothrops* demonstrates how several species have evolved from the same ancestor.

Jararaca (*Bothrops jajaraca*)

This is another big viper with large, angular blotches on its body. It resembles the barba amarilla and the jararacussu (see below). An inhabitant of grasslands it is one of the most abundant venomous snakes in South America.

Range: Southern Brazil, northeastern Paraguay, northern Argentina.

Danger Rating: High. Disturbed, it can be highly aggressive.

Remarks: While the jararaca does not produce a huge amount of highly toxic venom, within its range it is second only to the neotropical rattlesnake as a mankiller, perhaps because it is so abundant.

Jararacussu (*Bothrops jararacussu*)

This snake is not a common species within its range, which may be fortunate for the people who live there, because it delivers a massive amount of venom with its bite. The jararacussu is a highly amphibious snake, seldom found far from rivers, lakes, and other bodies of water. Given its habitat, fish and other aquatic creatures are a mainstay of its diet.

Range: Southern Brazil, eastern Bolivia, Paraguay and northern Argentina.

Size: Three to four feet, sometimes slightly larger.

Danger Rating: High. Responsible for many fatalities, despite its scarcity.

Remarks: Another in the group of lance-headed pit vipers that has radiated in the American tropics, probably due to lack of competition from rattlesnakes.

Fer-de-lance (*Bothrops lanceolatus*)

Several lance-headed pit vipers in South America are called by the name fer-de-lance. The only snake that qualifies for the name is one that lives in the West Indian island of Martinique. It is a typical pit viper, with blotches on its sides. As its name implies, it is a lance-headed viper. The fer-de-lance is a terrestrial species that once roamed the entire island but now is mainly confined to wilderness areas in forests.

Range: Martinique.

Size: It is a large snake, with some individuals exceeding seven feet.

Danger Rating: High. Very venomous.

Remarks: The only venomous snake on its island.

Neotropical rattlesnake (*Crotalus durissus*)

Also known as the cascabel, the neotropical rattlesnake is the only rattlesnake in South America, although it has a close relative, the Aruba rattlesnake, on the island of that name. This rattlesnake also inhabits Central America and southern Mexico, where, because of its skin pattern, it is sometimes mistaken for a western diamondback. This is the only rattlesnake on the mainland south of Mexico. A close relative, the Aruba rattlesnake (*Crotalus unicolor*) inhabits the West Indian island of Aruba.

This rattlesnake inhabits dry areas, grasslands and thorn scrub. It is exceedingly dangerous, delivering large quantities of venom that is even more toxic than that of the diamondbacks. Production of effective antivenin to combat the bites of this rattlesnake is difficult. Vast quantities of antivenin are required to treat bites. The bite of the neotropical rattlesnake wreaks havoc on body systems, causing blindness, paralysis and stopping respiration and heartbeat.

Range: Southern Mexico to northern Argentina.

Size: Maximum length six feet.

Danger Rating: Extreme.

Remarks: The toxicity of venom varies throughout this snake's range. It is most toxic in Brazil, where it is the main cause of snakebite fatalities.

Bushmaster (*Lachesis mutus*)

The bushmaster is a massive, big snake with a name that inspires fear. Tales abound of people dying within moments of a bushmaster bite. Indeed, a bushmaster bite could easily be lethal because of its long fangs, size and the large amount of venom delivered. On the other hand, bushmaster bites are rarely recorded, and known fatalities are even fewer. The main reason for the scarcity of dangerous encounters between the bushmaster and humans is that this snake is secretive and lives in the depths of tropical forests. It is active by night, when few people are likely to be treading forest paths. Moreover, despite its fearsome reputation, the bushmaster is not an aggressive snake. It is far less likely to strike, for example, than are most rattlesnakes. Even so, one would not want to be on the receiving end of a bushmaster's fangs, especially far from sources of treatment.

Range: Southern Nicaragua through the Amazon Basin.

Size: About seven feet, although specimens close to 12 feet have been reported.

Danger Rating: High, would be higher if it came into contact with people more often.

Remarks: The bushmaster has a distinctive burr of pointed spines near the tip of its tail.

Europe (and Western Asia)

FAMILY: VIPERIDAE

Adder (European viper) (*Vipera berus*)

The adder is the only snake to live north of the Arctic Circle. It has a variable ground color, from gray to yellow, but all specimens have a zigzag line down the back. In northern areas, it lives in habitat that is dry and open, exposed to the warming sun. In southern Europe, it favors mountains, where it can be found up to 9,000 feet high.

Range: Across Eurasia, from Sakhalin Island off Far Eastern Russia to Britain.

Size: Usually no more than two feet, sometimes up to 34 inches.

Danger Rating: Moderate. Fatalities are minimal.

Remarks: So well adapted to cold conditions that in spring it sometimes basks near snow.

Asp viper (*Vipera aspis*)

Confined to Europe, this small snake is similar in appearance to the adder. It is a hill-country snake, found up to altitudes of almost 8,000 feet. Rocky slopes of limestone and chalk, facing south to the sun, are its favorite habitat.

Range: Southern Europe from the Pyrenees to the Balkans, including Sicily.

Size: Two feet, occasionally slightly larger.

Danger Rating: Moderate. Bites seldom fatal but can take weeks to heal.

Remarks: Sluggish and not aggressive.

Sand viper (*Vipera ammodytes*)

Despite its name, this species is not a snake of desert dunes. It prefers dry, rocky country, although there it seeks out areas with sandy soil. This snake is also known as the long-nosed viper, perhaps a more appropriate name. The end of its snout is long and upturned, which helps it bulldoze through loose soil. Its color is variable, ranging from gray to pale orange. Like the rattlesnakes and other pit vipers of the Americas, European vipers display similar color patterns, evidence of subspeciation. The sand viper, like the adder, has a dark zigzag pattern down its back.

Range: Central and Southeastern Europe, through the Middle East into northern Iran.

Size: Usually a few inches less than a yard.

Danger Rating: Fairly high. Appears to be the European snake with the most toxic venom.

Remarks: This snake is terrestrial but often climbs into shrubs to bask.

Africa

FAMILY: COLUBRIDAE
Boomslang (*Dispholidus typus*)

Green in color, but oddly sometimes black, and living largely in shrubs and scattered trees, this bird-eater is a paradox. It is shy, running from danger rather than fighting. It is a rear-fanged snake, which means it has a venom delivery system that is less than efficient. But its venom is more toxic than that of African cobras and vipers, which says much about its danger to humans. The catch is that the boomslang must use the fangs in the rear of its jaw to chew its venom into its victim. It cannot strike quickly like a viper. If it could, it would be a true terror.

Range: Central and southern Africa.

Size: Usually four or five feet.

Danger Rating: High. While not aggressive, if it bites, the consequences can be deadly.

Remarks: Development of venom in colubrids, most of which are harmless, is evidence of how this trait has evolved in snakes.

FAMILY: ELAPIDAE
Black mamba (*Dendroaspix polylepis*)

With apologies to Australia's taipan, the black mamba is probably the top runner for the most dangerous snake in the world; although, certainly, the most dangerous of all is the one that bites you. It is one of four species of mamba in Africa, the rest of which are also menaces. In South Africa, the mamba is known as the "shadow of death." For a human that confronts it, this snake can indeed be the grim reaper. Although it spends some of its time in trees, it is swift as lightning on the ground, traveling at up to seven miles an hour overland. That is at least twice as fast as most snakes travel. With one strike, it can deliver enough venom to kill ten people. Roger Caras, in his book *Venomous Animals of the World*, notes that two drops of black mamba venom is a lethal dose for an average-sized human and large black mambas carry a load of up to 15 drops. Nervous and agile, the black mamba can strike for almost half of its length. Considering that many black mambas exceed 12 feet, this snake is definitely a long-range missile.

Range: Northeast Africa to South Africa.

Size: Nine or ten feet, but sometimes up to 14 feet. Very slim.

Danger Rating: Extreme. Unless antivenin is administered promptly, victims may die within minutes.

Remarks: Spreads its neck like a cobra when agitated.

Ringhals (*Hemachatus haemachatus*)

A cobra, the ringhals can spit its venom at the eyes of an enemy. Dark brown with light markings, it can spit for more than six feet with the accuracy of a true marksman. Spitting is a defensive measure, not used on potential prey. The ringhals inhabits bush country and savanna.

Range: Zimbabwe south to the Cape Province of South Africa.

Size: Three to four feet, sometimes larger.

Danger Rating: High. Venom in the eyes can cause blindness and the bite is often fatal.

Remarks: Venom "spit" is a fine spray. The spitting cobra (*Naja nigricolis*) is another, more widespread, cobra that ejects venomous spray through orifices in its fangs. The venom does not damage unbroken skin but, if in the eyes, causes tremendous damage. It must be flushed out with water or a similar fluid immediately. Zoo workers wear eye shields when dealing with this snake and the spitting cobra.

Egyptian cobra (*Naja haje*)

This is your typical cobra, which rears up with outspread hood when agitated. The posture is a warning rather than aggressive, and meant to ward off enemies. It is a very adaptable snake, living in a wide variety of habitats, such as agricultural fields, scrub and rocky hillsides. It shuns damp forests and interior deserts. Its color varies, from brown to yellowish.

Range: Northern three-quarters of Africa, Arabian Peninsula.

Size: About six feet, sometimes larger.

Danger Rating: High. Venom is very toxic, although this species is not unusually aggressive.

Remarks: The Egyptian cobra is probably the "asp" that Cleopatra used to commit suicide.

Forest cobra (*Naja melanoleuca*)

A big cobra, shiny black above, it is totally terrestrial. It is most common in rain forests but also lives in drier woodlands through much of its range. This is a retiring snake that avoids confrontation whenever it can, although if provoked it will vigorously defend itself. It is a slow-moving animal, to the point of being sluggish.

Range: West, Central and much of Southern Africa.
Size: Heavy bodied, up to eight feet long.
Danger Rating: High. Lack of aggression results in few bites but venom is very toxic.
Remarks: Sometimes mistaken for the much slimmer black mamba.

Yellow cobra (*Naja nivea*)

The yellow cobra possesses the most toxic venom of any cobra in Africa. It responds to a perceived threat quickly, rearing up and spreading its head in typical cobra fashion. Although it is immediately ready to strike, it will retreat if given the opportunity. Most yellow cobras are, as the name implies, yellowish in color, but coloration can range from rusty brown to black.

Range: Temperate areas of southern Africa to the Cape of South Africa. It is sometimes called the "Cape cobra."
Size: Usually about six feet.
Danger Rating: High, because of the toxicity of its venom, even though it is not particularly aggressive.
Remarks: In the event of a bite, antivenin must be administered quickly or death will result.

FAMILY: VIPERIDAE
Bibron's mole viper (*Atractaspis bibronii*)

This is one of a dozen species of mole vipers in Africa. Mole vipers hunt rodents and other small animals in their burrows. Their venomous fangs are on the sides of the jaw, rather than in front, as in other vipers. The fangs are adapted for a strike in the close confines of a burrow. Instead of striking forward, the mole viper hits downward and to the rear.

Range: Southern Africa, from Angola and Zimbabwe to South Africa.
Size: Usually less than two feet. Sometimes only 15 inches.

Danger Rating: Moderate. Bites are seldom if ever fatal but are very painful.

Remarks: Due to the retiring habits of mole vipers, most bites occur when people try to handle them.

Gaboon viper (*Bitis gabonica*)

The gaboon viper is a very sluggish snake that sleeps so deeply during the day that it is difficult to rouse. Even at night, it moves relatively slowly. This snake has a massive body, immense fangs, measuring up to two inches long, and a huge amount of highly toxic venom. A strike in a person's foot can drive the fangs all the way through it, causing severe physical, as well as chemical, damage. Envenomated blood from such a wound quickly spreads the infection.

Range: Tropical rain forests from Southern Sudan to northern South Africa.

Size: Up to six feet but has the heaviest body of any viper.

Danger Rating: High. Untreated bites are usually fatal. Because of its sluggish nature, bites are relatively rare.

Remarks: Leaf-like patterns on this viper's body make it difficult to see on the forest floor.

Rhinoceros viper (*Bitis nasicornis*)

The rhinoceros viper is another heavy-bodied viper of Africa. Its name comes from the fact that it has two or three horny projections on its snout. The gaboon viper may also have these projections. A dark, arrow-shaped marking on the head of the rhinoceros viper is a key distinguishing mark between the two species. The rhinoceros viper inhabits moist areas—swamps, river banks, and lakesides within the African rain forest.

Range: Liberia through Central Africa.

Size: About three feet, with a stout body.

Danger Rating: High. Venom is very toxic and the snake is aggressive.

Remarks: The rhinoceros viper is also known as the "river jack."

Puff adder (*Bitis arietans*)

Almost as massive as the Gaboon viper, the puff adder probably kills more Africans than any other snake. There are several reasons for this. It has an immense range; its coloration, dark and light markings, blends into the ground cover, so it is difficult to see; and it often prowls around human dwellings at night as it searches for rodents. The puff adder also rivals the Gaboon viper in the length of its fangs and power of its venom. Another trait of the puff adder that makes it such a man killer is that when approached, it does not flee but holds its ground, putting unwary walkers in harm's way.

Range: Through most of Africa in savannah and grasslands. Also western Arabia.

Size: Three to four feet.

Danger Rating: Very high. Bites cause enormous tissue damage and swelling and, even if treated, can be fatal within 24 hours.

Remarks: The puff adder and Gaboon viper are closely related snakes with similar habits. They seldom compete because the puff adder is a species of open country while the Gaboon viper is an animal of deep forest.

Southern Asia

FAMILY: ELAPIDAE
Indian krait (*Bungarus caeruleus*)

Along with the black mamba and Australian taipan (to be described), the Indian krait ranks as one of the most dangerous snakes in the world. Kraits in general—a dozen species are recognized—are all extremely dangerous. Inhabiting southeast Asia, kraits are not well known for their lethal qualities outside of the realm in which they live. Westerners tend to think of the cobra, head raised and hood spread, as the most frightening of Asian snakes. Not so the locals. For a good reason, they call kraits the "Seven step snakes," which means that is as far as you go after being bitten before dying.

Kraits get little press outside of their world because they are rather timid, secretive snakes, hiding in the day but prowling for prey at night. They are rather ordinary looking and resemble many non-venomous snakes. The Indian krait is dark brown or black with narrow white or yellow crossbands. Kraits, which feed mostly on other snakes, have a very toxic venom. The impact of an Indian krait's bite is particularly lethal. Four milligrams of venom are usually fatal, and are so even in more than 50 percent of cases that have been treated. Living mostly in dry open country, the Indian krait is especially active on warm, humid nights.

An exception to the lethal nature of kraits is the banded krait, which lives throughout much of southern Asia. It is so docile that many people believe it is harmless. When alarmed, it seldom tries to bite. Instead, it hides its head in its coils, as if hoping danger will go away.

Range: India and nearby areas.
Size: Less than five feet.
Danger Rating: High, if it strikes.
Remarks: "Krait" is a Hindi word.

Asiatic cobra (*Naja naja*)

Many people associate cobras more with Asia than Africa. Actually, Africa has the largest number of cobra species. Southern Asia has many cobras but, although taxonomists have divided them into a half dozen subspecies, all are the same species (*Naja naja*) under the skin. (The lone outsider is the king cobra, which belongs to an entirely different genus.)

The Asiatic cobra, in its various forms, has a huge range, from the Middle East to Southern China, and the Philippines, as well as southern areas of Asiatic Russia. The most widespread subspecies is the Indian cobra. Color differs with the subspecies, ranging from olive to black. Some Asiatic cobras, such as the Indian subspecies, have spectacle markings on back of the hood.

Asiatic cobras are highly adaptable snakes and live in many types of habitat, excluding desert and deep rain forest. Level terrain with high grass and scattered bunches of trees suits them best. Agricultural land, such as rice paddies, often attract cobras, which also can be common in towns and cities, where they search for rats and other rodents. Cobra bites are frequent, especially in India, because cobras and humans often come into contact. Ironically, however, biting is often a last-ditch defense; cobras sometimes strike with mouth closed. When they do bite, they hang on, chewing viciously. Asiatic cobra venom is quite toxic, but there is evidence that they may use only small quantities of venom when striking defensively. Many human victims recover without treatment.

Range: Middle East through southern Asia to south China, including Taiwan, Borneo and the Philippines.

Size: Four or five feet, sometimes slightly larger.

Danger Rating: High.

Remarks: Some subspecies are known to spit venom, but infrequently.

King cobra (*Ophiophagus hannah*)

The largest venomous snake, the king cobra is undeniably dangerous, but has a much worse reputation than it deserves. Certainly, a cobra that can rear up so high that it can almost look a man in the eye, and pump out a vast amount of venom, is a formidable and daunting creature. However, its habits make encounters with people, and bites in humans, exceedingly rare. The king cobra, which lives in both woodlands and open country, is not an abundant snake. Its diet is almost exclusively other snakes, so it seldom prowls around human habitation, as do Asiatic cobras that are hunting rats. Because of its diet, its venom is less toxic to mammals than that of the Asiatic cobra, although it is more toxic to reptiles. Even so, because of its immense size, up to 18 feet, if the king cobra does bite it can produce a flood of venom so, under the right (or, perhaps, wrong) circumstances, it is a lethal customer.

Range: India east to southern China and south to Indonesia and the Philippines.

Size: Usually from seven to 13 feet but often larger.

Danger Rating: High, especially if cornered.

Remarks: The female is the only snake to build a true nest, of decaying leaves and other vegetation, for herself and her eggs. Some female king cobras vigorously defend their nests, which is when they may be more aggressive than normally.

FAMILY: VIPERIDAE
Russell's viper (*Vipera Russelii*)

Like the Asiatic cobra, Russell's viper often seeks out rats in agricultural fields and around buildings. It prefers habitats that are grassy or brushy, often at elevations up to 7,000 feet. It is a slow moving snake but counterattacks quickly when threatened. This viper varies in ground color from deep yellow to olive. Its back is covered with round spots, rimmed by black.

Range: India to southeastern China, south to Indonesia.
Size: Approximately four to five feet.
Danger Rating: High. Cases of many bites but venom is not as toxic to humans as that of kraits and the Asiatic cobra.
Remarks: Some females can produce up to 60 young.

McMahon's viper (*Eristicophis macmahonii*)

Also called the Asian sand viper, this snake is a typical desert viper, with a flattened body and tan skin. Its habits are little known. Sand dunes are one of its favorite habitats.
Range: Iran to Pakistan.
Size: Usually less than three feet.
Danger Rating: Considerable, if encountered. Its bite has been recoded as fatal.
Remarks: Many Eurasian pit vipers of deserts are very similar in appearance and habits, evidence of a common origin.

Malayan pit viper (*Agistrodon rhodostoma*)

A relative of the North American cottonmouth and copperhead, the Malayan pit viper has a nasty disposition and, when disturbed, gives little or no notice before striking. In some parts of Southeast Asia, it causes hundreds of bites a year, partly because it is extremely common on rubber plantations, where workers often encounter it. It is rosy colored on the back, with dark crossbands.
Range: Southeast Asia, Thailand to Sumatra and Java.
Size: About three feet.
Danger Rating: High because of frequent bites; fatalities, however, are minimum.
Remarks: The female guards her eggs.

Pope's tree viper (*Trimeresurus popeiorum*)

The Pope's tree viper is one of several species of small, slender arboreal vipers that inhabit southern Asia. These vipers are members of the lance-headed pit vipers group. Most of these vipers, like Pope's, are green and slender, with prehensile tails. They seldom visit the ground.
Range: Southeast Asia to Indonesia.
Size: About three feet.

Danger Rating: Moderate. Bites are painful but seldom, if ever, fatal.

Okinawa habu (*Trimeresurus flavoviridis*)

This species is another lance-headed pit viper. It is terrestrial, roaming the cultivated fields and palm forest. It is most common at the boundary between the two habitats, where the so-called "edge effect"—animal life, and thus prey, is especially abundant at interfaces between habitats—takes hold. The habu seeks shelter in rock areas, such as caves, walls, and even old tombs. The habu often enters human dwellings and other building as it hunts for rodents.

Range: Amami and Okinawa Islands.

Size: Usually around four feet, sometimes more than seven feet.

Danger Rating: High. Because it often encounters people, and is quite aggressive, the habu is responsible for a large number of bites within its range. Its venom is not highly toxic, so only about three percent of bites are fatal. However, up to eight percent of its victims suffer permanent disability.

Remarks: A close relative is the Chinese habu (*Trimeresurus mucosquamatus*), which lives from southern China and Taiwan to Viet Nam and Laos.

FAMILY: HYDROPHIIDAE

Amphibious sea snake (*Laticauda colubrina*)

This is a rather primitive member of the sea snake subfamily, the Laticudines. Typical of sea snakes, its tail is horizontally flattened for propulsion. Unlike the majority of sea snakes, however, this species is able to move fairly well on land, where it lays its eggs.

Range: Eastern Indo-Pacific, from India to Japan and south to Australia.

Size: About four feet.

Danger Rating: High if contacted, but sea people rarely encounter sea snakes.

Remarks: This species is said to sometimes enter fishing villages and steal fish set out to dry.

Yellow-bellied sea snake (*Pelamis platurus*)

The yellow-bellied sea snake has the largest range of any snake. It can be found throughout the entire tropical and subtropical Indo-Pacific. It is completely pelagic, never leaving the water. Like other sea snakes it feeds on fish.

Range: Indo-Pacific from Japan and Australia to East Africa and Central and South America.

Danger Rating: High if contacted.

Remarks: Females bear live young in shallow inlets.

Australia (including major Pacific Islands)

FAMILY: ELAPIDAE

Death adder (*Acanthophis antarcticus*)

European settlers of Australia christened this elapid snake an "adder" because outwardly it closely resembles a viper, with a broad, flat head distinct from the neck and a blunt snout. This snake also exhibits behavior that is more typical of vipers than it is of elapids. It is a widespread snake, found in many habitats, from dry scrub to tropical rain forests and deserts, except for the driest and hottest. Like many vipers, it often hides in the sand during the day, when it is seldom active. The death adder hunts small mammals and birds mainly at night. The behavior of a death adder that feels threatened is like that of many vipers. It does not retreat, but flattens out, then strikes with a speed possessed by few elapids.

Range: Most of Australia, also New Guinea and nearby islands.

Size: No more than two feet.

Danger Rating: Extreme. Its aggressive defense and highly toxic venom make it one of the most dangerous snakes in Australia, perhaps anywhere. Without proper medical care, a victim has up to a 50-percent chance of dying.

Remarks: There is at least one other species of death adder (*Acanthophis pyrrhus*), which is rare and localized. Taxonomists argue whether or not there are more species than two in this group. However, given the death adder's wide range, they may be subspecies.

Australian brown snake (*Demansia textilis*)

Despite its name, the brown snake can range in color from brown to grayish tan. It is an extremely abundant snake, tolerating habitats ranging from wheat and rice fields to scrub. When threatened, it is aggressive, flattening its neck, looping its body into an S shape, and raising its head. This behavior evokes faint images of the cobra, although the brown snake does not rear up its head more than a few inches off the ground and lacks a true hood. Even so, the brown snake is sometimes called the "false cobra." The brown snake is extremely fast and very agile.

Range: Much of Australia and eastern New Guinea.

Size: Usually five to six feet, sometimes larger.

Danger Rating: Extreme, due to its abundance, size, speed and aggressive disposition and strikes repeatedly. It causes more deaths than any other Australian snake.

Remarks: Some taxonomists consider that brown snakes with geographical variations are individual species.

Australian yellow-spotted snake (*Hoplocephalus bungaroides*)

This is a dark brown or black snake, with yellow spots that create crossbands or a netting on the body. Nocturnal, it often is found on rocky slopes and in coastal areas. It frequently ascends trees.

Range: Southern Queensland and New South Wales.

Size: Three to four feet, but sometimes larger.

Danger Rating: Fairly high. Bites cause vomiting, pain, problems with vision and breathing, and sometimes bleeding from the gums. According to the Navy manual, *Poisonous Snakes of the World,* the bite of a large specimen could be lethal.

Remarks: Accounts say that the Australian yellow-spotted snake is aggressive and may attack without provocation.

Australian tiger snake (*Notechis scutatus*)

One species of this snake is generally recognized, although it has several distinct geographic races. The snake gets its name from its coloration, a yellow-to-cream background color ringed with broad, gray bands. One variation is completely black, and some scientists consider it as a separate species. The tiger snake is a creature of wet habitats, especially those that are rocky and brushy. It is active by night, and most bites occur when people tread upon it.

Range: Southern Australia and Tasmania.

Size: Four to five feet but sometimes larger.

Danger Rating: Extreme. The tiger snake has highly toxic venom that causes a host of systemic reactions, including respiratory paralysis and circulatory failure. Untreated bites are likely to be lethal.

Remarks: One of the most frequent causes of snakebite in Australia.

Taipan (*Oxyuranus scutellatus*)

Many scientists consider that this snake may be the deadliest on Earth, at least as lethal as the black mamba. It is a huge snake, rivaling the king cobra and bushmaster in length. With fangs more than a half inch long—large for an elapid—and the ability to introduce a massive dose of venom that is among the most toxic existing, the taipan is a genuine man killer. Even after antivenin is administered, recovery chances may be poor. Fortunately, the taipan is a relatively rare species, found mostly in isolated areas, generally with low human populations, so encounters are infrequent. Few people have ever seen one. In fact, the taipan was not discovered until 1867, when one was killed in Queensland. Additional specimens were not obtained until a half century later. When it attacks, the taipan moves like a flash, often biting several times before a victim can react. Rocky areas in grassland are its preferred habitat. Body color is coppery or brown to grayish black.

Range: Northern Australia and parts of coastal New Guinea.

Size: Up to 11 feet.

Danger Rating: Extreme. Before antivenin was developed, death from a taipan bite was virtually certain. Even with treatment, survival can be uncertain. The venom is neurotoxic, causing several systemic symptoms, including respiratory failure.

Remarks: The taipan has a frightening defensive display. It flattens its head and forebody to the ground, arches its back and lashes its tail.

Australian mulga snake (Black Snake) (*Pseudechis australis*)

A large snake, brown in color, this species is sometimes mistaken for the much more dangerous taipan. It is an inhabitant of dry regions, where it can be common.

Range: Northern Australia and southern New Guinea.
Size: Up to nine feet.
Danger Rating: High, because when it bites it holds on and chews in venom. However, the venom is moderately toxic and seldom kills.
Remarks: This snake holds its ground when disturbed.

Representative Giant Snakes
New World

FAMILY: BOIDAE
Boa constrictor (*Boa constrictor*)

The boa constrictor, like other members of its family, is a relatively primitive snake. However, it is highly adaptable, successful and abundant through a vast area of the American tropics and subtropics. Its survival ability is demonstrated by the fact that the boa constrictor is one of the easiest snakes to maintain in captivity—and by the fact that captive specimens are readily available because this snake breeds easily under human care. The boa constrictor is so abundant that it is often called "the common boa." It is "common" only because it succeeds where other snakes may not.

The range of the boa constrictor spans most of Latin America. It is as much at home in the lower levels of forest as it is on the ground. It feeds mostly on warm-blooded animals, but within that category, it has an extensive diet, from small and mid-size rodents to birds that it finds both on the ground and in the lower branches of the forest.

Boa constrictors are mainly a species inhabiting tropical rain forest, but they also thrive in many habitats that are quite different. In some parts of Central America, there are what scientists call "dry rain forests," subject to heavy seasonal rains but with soil that leaches out water rapidly, creating arid soil. Boas live in these places as well, as they do in some regions of semi-arid scrub.

Range: Northwestern Mexico to Argentina. Also on islands off the east coast of Central and South America. Including islets off Honduras, Trinidad, Tobago and St. Lucia.

Size: A boa constrictor of 10 feet is considered large. But some of these snakes reach 18 feet.

Remarks: The boa constrictor is the snake seen most often in jungle movies, slithering out of trees to confront heroes and heroines. No wonder. It is big, impressive but docile. The boa constrictor is the best giant snake for use by an animal handler.

Anaconda (*Eunectes murinus*)

The anaconda is the snake of legends; some of which are based on truth, but many on hearsay. The anaconda, sometimes called the "green anaconda," to distinguish it from a smaller species (or subspecies, depending on which taxonomy is accepted), the yellow anaconda (*Eunectes notaeus*). The anaconda is seldom if ever found far from water. It spends most of its time in rivers and swampy areas. One of the optimum habitats for the anaconda is the Caroni Swamp of Trinidad. This island, a few miles off the coast of Venezuela, is close enough to the South American continent that it has a largely South American fauna—howler monkeys and macaws, for instance. The Caroni is a fresh and brackish swamp, with tangles of mangroves and channels that lace through brushy swamp vegetation. Many years ago, before it became a tourist attraction because of the flocks of scarlet ibises that feed there, I traversed the swamp. I will confess that I never saw an anaconda (they can be secretive) but seeing its haunts gives one an idea of how it hunts. The anaconda hides in low water and seizes prey that lives there or comes to water's edge for a drink. Mammals, such as the capybara, reptiles, including small caimans and turtles, are high on its dietary list. Typically, it drags its prey under water and kills by constriction.

Range: Most of tropical South America.

Size: May approach 30 feet, perhaps more.

Remarks: Probably the most powerful snake in the world. Although accounts are not well documented, it can be a predator upon humans.

Old World

FAMILY: BOIDAE

Reticulated python (*Python reticulatus*)

This snake competes with the anaconda for the title of the world's longest snake, but even so it lacks the mass of the South American giant. The netted patterns on its body make it distinctive. The reticulated python is generally a forest snake, although it may be found in grassy areas and scrub as well. It is the largest snake in Asia.

Range: Southeast Asia and Australasian islands such as Celebes.

Size: May approach 30 feet, perhaps even larger.

Remarks: By some accounts, this snake has occasionally preyed upon humans. It certainly is large enough to do so.

Indian python (*Python molurus*)

The second-largest snake in Asia is the Indian python. It shares some of its range with the reticulated python but is distinguished from the former by its skin pattern, which is marked by oblong brown blotches edged in black. It is also smaller than the reticulated species. Like the reticulated python, this species is essentially a forest animal. However, it sometimes ranges into grassland and scrub.

Range: India, Burma, Sri Lanka adjacent areas.

Size: Usually in the neighborhood of a dozen feet but can reach approximately 20 feet.

Remarks: The Burmese form is a subspecies (*Python molorus bivittatus*).

African rock python (*Python sebae*)

This is the only snake in Africa that qualifies as a true giant. It is found in bush, savanna and forests. It frequently enters the water. Like the above-mentioned pythons it feeds on mammals and birds.

Range: Africa, south of the Sahara.

Size: Up to 25 feet, usually smaller.

Remarks: The African rock python is known to go for more than two years without eating. Between fasts, it feeds voraciously. Snakes that consume large prey are often able to go for long periods between meals, but the rock python is truly remarkable in this respect.

Amethystine python (*Morelia amethistina*)

This large python inhabits several types of habitats, from desert scrub to tropical forest. In Australia, it is also called the scrub python, a name that suggests where it is most commonly found. The numbers of this species were severely depleted by skin hunters prior to World War II, sparking Australia to introduce some of the first conservation laws protecting giant snakes.

Range: Northern Australia and New Guinea.

Size: Variable. Many are up to a dozen feet long but some over 20 feet long have been reported.

Remarks: This python can have an aggressive temperament.

Representative Non-Venomous Snakes
North America

FAMILY: COLUBRIDAE
Worm snake (*Carphophis amoneus*)

This little burrowing snake not only eats mainly earthworms, but might be mistaken for one from above. Its back is brown to black in coloration, although it has a rosy pink belly. As one might expect from its diet, it is often found in the same places as worms—moist spots under rocks, in rotting logs and in loose soil. During dry periods, it often burrows deeply into the soil. Worm snakes are quite secretive and at least partly nocturnal, so they are seldom seen. Like frogs, toads and salamanders, they often cross roads on humid or rainy nights. In addition to worms, their diet includes small salamanders and insects, especially larvae. There are three subspecies, eastern (*C. a. amoneus*), midwestern (*C. a. helenae*) and western (*C. a. vermis*).

Range: Much of the eastern and central United States, from southern New England to Georgia and west to eastern Oklahoma.

Size: Seven to about 10 inches.

Remarks: When picked up this snake often flattens its head or tail against the hand, and tries to wedge its way out of restraint.

Indigo snake (*Drymarchon corais*)

This is one of the most impressive snakes of the Americas. It is big, fast, and, when need be, furious. As snakes go, it is rather primitive. It has no venom and cannot constrict. It kills prey, ranging from frogs and small mammals to rattlesnakes, by a powerful strike of its jaws. It is an elegant snake, glossy dark-blue in color, which inhabits a vast portion of the Americas. In the United States, there are two forms, the eastern indigo snake (*D. c. couperi*) and the Texas subspecies (*D. c. erebennus*). Both are creatures of dry areas but like to live near water.

Range: The eastern subspecies lives from southern Georgia to the Florida Keys. The Texas subspecies ranges from southern Texas well into Mexico. Other subspecies range well into South America.

Racer (*Coluber constrictor*)

The racer is one of the most widespread snakes in North America. There are about a dozen different subspecies, although taxonomists do not agree on the exact number. There is a fair amount of color variation among these subspecies. The type subspecies is the northern black racer (*C. c. constrictor*), dark black in color. Other subspecies include the tan racer (*C. c. etheridgei*), which is light tan, and the Everglades racer (*C. c. paludicola*), which is bluish green to brownish gray. Large but slim, racers, as their name implies, are fast, agile snakes that literally streak along the ground when fully on the move. They are also excellent climbers. During hunting forays, they travel with heads raised. Racers feed on a wide variety of prey, ranging from large insects to birds and, often, other snakes. Specimens collected in Connecticut contained in their digestive tract wood frogs, ring-necked snakes, and brown snakes. The wide range of the racer testifies to the fact that it can live in many different habitats, including grassland, open woodland, and mountains up to 7,000 feet in altitude.

Range: Every state in the continental United States except Alaska and the southern margins of Ontario and British Columbia. South to Guatemala.

Size: Three to about six feet.

Remarks: When aroused, the racer coils and often strikes repeatedly. It also vibrates its tail, which in dry leaves makes a sound like a rattlesnake's buzz. Not a few people have been frightened out of their wits by this behavior.

Ringneck snake (*Diadophis punctatus*)

This is a small, very slender little snake that is extremely attractive. Of the dozen subspecies, most have a dark back, black, gray or brownish and a neck ring, of yellow, cream or orange. The belly is orange, yellow or red. The type species is southern ringneck (*D.P. punctatus*). Ringneck snakes utilize an even wider spectrum of habitats than racers, including disturbed areas such as dumps and gravel pits. Natural habitats include moist deciduous woodland and desert, hemlock forests and pine barrens and, often, suburban backyards. Ringnecks are relatively secretive, often hiding under fallen logs, flat rocks and slabs of bark. Young ringneck snakes, pencil thin, sometimes creep under doors and enter houses.

Range: Nova Scotia to Florida, west to New Mexico and eastern Arizona. Scattered populations west of that, including a contiguous range along the Pacific coast. Absent from much of the High Plains. South into Mexico.

Size: 10 to 30 inches.

Remarks: When threatened some ringnecks coil the tail and raise it to expose the bright color of its underside. This is a display designed to distract the interloper. When handled, ringnecks may release a smelly goo from the cloaca.

Pine snake (*Pituophis melanoleucus*)

Scientists once classified the pine snake and the gopher snake as two different species. The opinion changed; nowadays, this species is known as the pine-gopher snake. The dual names come from the serpent's habitat and prey. It often lives in piney woods, although it can be found on prairies and even semi-desert. It preys largely on rodents, especially gophers, in whose burrows it sometimes seeks refuge.

This snake is mostly active by day. It has 15 geographical races, some of which range into Mexico. There are several color variations between species.

Range: Middle Atlantic to Florida. Most of the United States west of the Mississippi.

Size: Can be 10 feet long.

Remarks: When threatened, it often vibrates its tail, imitating a rattlesnake.

Corn snake (*Elaphe guttata*)

The corn snake, named for a belly skin pattern that resembles an ear of Indian corn, is one of the all-time favorites of people who keep snakes as pets. It is a hardy, docile snake of considerable beauty, and has lived in captivity for more than 20 years. Experts on keeping snakes often recommend this species as one of the best for beginners. There are two subspecies of corn snakes; the corn snake, proper (*E. g. guttata*) and the Great Plains rat snake (*E.g. emoryi*). The Great Plains species is not a true rat snake (see following) but both corn snakes and rat snakes belong to the same genus, and so are very similar. Common names often do not follow the distinctions of scientific terminology.

This is a snake of relatively open areas, such as meadows, scattered woodlands and farmyards. It often prowls around farm buildings in search of prey—small rodents, birds, and bats. It can reach roosting bats because it is a good climber. Corn snakes are orange to orange-brown in background color. Blotches—red, brown or gray and edged in red—run down the back. The belly pattern that gives this snake its name is lighter in color than the back and has square black markings running in rows, head to tail.

Range: Southern New Jersey into Florida, west to New Mexico. Also into Mexico.

Size: Two to six feet, but rarely maximum size.

Remarks: During the late 1990s, a reptile collector picked up a corn snake in the California desert, far from the natural range of the species. It was obviously a specimen that had been released by or had escaped from a collector.

Rat snake (*Elaphe obsoleta*)

There are six species of true rat snakes, most typical of which is the black rat snake (*E. o. obsoleta*). Like the king snake, the rat snake has evolved some marked coloration differences between snakes from distinct geographical ranges. The black rat snake, which lives from central New England south to Georgia and west to the Midwest, is as its name suggests, unmarked black. Other subspecies vary considerably in color. The Everglades rat snake (*E. o. rossalleni*), of the southern tip of Florida, is reddish orange with four barely discernible dark stripes.

Big and powerful, rat snakes are constrictors that feed on birds and their eggs, mammals and an occasional lizard. They are adept climbers that frequently raid bird nests. Some birds, hawks, for instance, turn the tables and prey on rat snakes.

Range: Central New England to the Florida Keys, west to Minnesota, Oklahoma and Indiana.

Size: Three feet to about eight feet.

Remarks: When ranges overlap, the rat snake often overwinters in the same dens as copperheads and timber rattlers. It usually emerges first in the spring.

Eastern hognose snake (*Heterodon platyrhinos*)

This species is the best known and most widespread of the hognose snakes. There are two other species in North America, the western hognose (*H. nasicus*) of the Great Plains and the southern hognose (*H. simus*) of the Southeast. The eastern hognose is famed for its defensive displays. It tries at first to mimic a venomous snake in defensive posture and behavior. If that does not work, it rolls over and plays dead, but rolls over again if overturned. This snake, which lives mainly in open areas with predominately sandy soil, is one reason why one of its strongholds is Cape Cod. The eastern hognose preys almost exclusively on toads, usually American toads, although it will not turn down a tasty frog or salamander. Its name comes from its flat, upturned snout.

Range: Minnesota and Central New England to Florida, west to Texas and Kansas.

Remarks: Increasingly, evidence has mounted that the hognose can deliver venom of slight toxicity via its rear fangs. It is not considered even a minimal threat to people.

Coachwhip (*Masticophis flagellum*)

Legend has it that this snake uses its body, in shape the serpentine version of a bullwhip, to beat its foes to death. It is not true, of course. When threatened this big snake coils and then strikes repeatedly. Unusually flexible even for a snake, with a long tail, this snake moves lightning-fast. John L. Behler and F. Wayne King, noted herpetologists and authors of *The Audubon Society Field Guide to North American Reptiles and Amphibians*, write that the coachwhip may be the fastest North American snake. As with many other colubrids listed here, the coachwhip has several subspecies. Most, including the Sonora (*M. f. Cingulum*) and the Baja California (*M. f. fulginosus*), range into Mexico.

The coachwhip is a snake of dry, open areas, such as pine flatwoods, prairies and desert scrub. It feeds on large insects, lizards, snakes and small rodents.

Range: Southeast North Carolina and southwestern Tennessee to Florida; west to Colorado, and through the Southwest to southern California. Also into Mexico.

Size: Three feet to about eight feet.

Remarks: Often shelters in mammal burrows.

Northern water snake (*Nerodia sipedon*)

A robust snake with an aggressive temperament, the northern watersnake is victim of misidentification. People often mistake it for the venomous cottonmouth, or "water moccasin," even well outside the range of the latter, and resultantly, kill it. The water snake's willingness to fight an aggressor, and bite, does not help its case. When angered, it also discharges a foul-smelling secretion from anal glands.

The confusion with the cottonmouth stems from the water snake's coloration; brownish with dark markings and its habitat. Like the cottonmouth, the water snake is found in and around streams, ponds, wetlands and similar aquatic situations. It is hardy, even able to live in urban areas. They are common, for example, in many New York City parks. Northern water snakes subsist primarily on aquatic prey, largely fish but also frogs, salamanders and, occasionally, small turtles. There are four subspecies.

Range: Maine to the Carolinas, west to Louisiana and eastern Colorado.

Size: Two to four feet.

Remarks: Saliva contains an anti-coagulant, which makes wounds bleed extensively.

Common garter snake (*Thamnophis sirtalis*)

Usually found near water—roadside ditches as well as large lakes and streams—this species has the greatest distribution of any snake in North America. It is the snake most frequently seen in many of the areas it inhabits, because it is so abundant and is active by day. It has 13 subspecies. The type species is the eastern (*T. s. sirtalis*), which has three longitudinal stripes, often yellow, down its back. Throughout its range, however, the common garter snake shows considerable color variation. Most colorful of the garter snakes is the San Francisco species (*T. s. tetrataenia*), which is confined largely to the San Francisco Peninsula. It has a greenish-yellow dorsal stripe, which is edged in black, and paralleled on each side by a red stripe, which is bordered by one of black. The top of its head is bright red. It is highly endangered. Garter snakes feed on cold-blooded creatures that inhabit moist areas; frogs, toads, and salamanders. They often eat small fish as well.

Range: Southern Canada to the Gulf, coast to coast, except for Southwestern deserts.

Size: 18 inches to about four feet maximum. Most of those encountered are at the low end of the size spectrum.

Remarks: Although still common, garter snakes are vulnerable to wetlands destruction.

Mexico and Central America
FAMILY: COLUBRIDAE
Sonoran shovel-nosed snake (*Chionactis palarostris*)

Like many snakes of Mexico, this species ranges into the border region of the United States. However, as its name suggests, the majority of its range is in Sonora, Mexico. Its name also indicates its habitat; desert. The flattened snout of this snake enables it to burrow into the sand for shelter and in search of the invertebrates upon which it feeds. Like many other burrowing snakes, it is quite small.

Range: Sonora, Mexico into extreme south-central Arizona. The race in Arizona is called the Organ Pipe (*C. p. organica*) after the Organ Pipe Cactus National Park.

Size: Ten to 15 inches.

Remarks: Little is known about its habits because it is a burrower and nocturnal.

Speckled racer (*Drymobius margaritiferus*)

Not closely related to the *Coluber* racers, this snake is close kin to the indigo snakes. It is a slim snake, black with a green tinge. It has yellow spots—soectacles—on its dorsal scales. This snake lives in brushy areas near water and feeds on amphibians, mostly frogs.

Range: Mostly south of the American border to northern South America. Into the extreme south of Texas.

Size: Three to four feet.

Remarks: Even though some of its habitat is nominally dry, it concentrates on watercourses and water holes where it can find its prey.

Mexican hook-nosed snake (*Ficimia streckeri*)

This is another snake with a snout modified for burrowing in soil—its nose hooks upwards into a point. It has a curious range. It lives in desert and desert scrub, but also in mountain forests up to almost 5,000 feet. These forests are called "cloud forests," because they are very wet and regularly cloaked in fog, mist and rain. Little is known about this snake, which feeds largely on arachnids, such as spiders.

Range: Northern Mexico, edging into the border region of Texas.

Size: Very small. Nine inches to about 18 inches.

Remarks: The western hook-nosed snake (*Gyalopion canum*), which has a largely similar habitat range, is even smaller. It can reach a length of only eight inches.

Mexican vine snake (*Oxybelis aeneus*)

This snake is interesting because it is highly arboreal, yet unlike most other tree snakes it is not primarily an inhabitant of rain forest. Rather, it lives mostly in low, arid forest dominated by brush and low oaks, although at the southern end of its range it extends into rain forests. Its coloration, brown to gray, reflects its preferred habitat. Tree snakes restricted to rain forests are generally green. This species is one of several colubrid snakes of

Mexico and the Southwestern United States that have rear fangs that introduce a mild venom. They are considered "harmless" because the venom is not truly dangerous to people and, moreover, to be bitten, a person would almost have to jam a finger down the serpent's throat. However, the venom paralyzes the lizards and other reptiles upon which the vine snake feeds.

Range: Mexico to Brazil, touches the southernmost margins of Arizona.

Chihuahuan black-headed snake (*Tantilla wilcoxi*)

This light-brown snake gets its name from the striking black cap on its head. It is another burrower, feeding on invertebrates such as spiders and insect larvae. It is a snake of dry grasslands, but ascends mountains into coniferous forests, up to almost a mile in altitude.

Range: Northern Mexico, edges into Arizona.
Remarks: It is active by night.

Guatemalan indigo snake (*Drymarchon*)

Similar to the indigo snakes of the United States, this species, like its northern relatives, is mainly a serpent of open country, including savannas. It is a voracious predator. Harry W. Greene, in his book *Snakes, The Evolution of Mystery in Nature*, refers to one of these snakes, over six feet long, that was seen swallowing a boa constrictor half its length.

Range: Central America.
Size: Up to more than eight feet.
Remarks: In parts of the American tropics, indigo snakes are called "Sababeras" meaning "savanna animals."

South America and the West Indies

FAMILY: ANILIIDAE
South American Pipe Snake (*Anilius scytale*)

Because of its coloration, this species is also known as the false coral snake and the red-tailed pipe snake. It is a brilliantly colored snake, with reddish-orange and black rings on its body.

This color pattern resembles that of venomous coral snakes, which are banded by rings of red and black, separated by yellow, an example of warning coloration. The mimicry of the pipe snake may help protect it from predators. It can also have the opposite result. People may kill it, thinking it is dangerous. The pipe snake lives mainly in rain forests. It seeks its prey—other small snakes and amphibians—by burrowing into the soil and in the water.

Range: The Amazon Basin area.

Size: About three feet.

Remarks: This is the only species in its family, although some scientists assign it to the family Uropeltidae (pipe snakes and shield-tailed snakes), which is native to Asia.

FAMILY: BOIDAE

Rainbow boa (*Epicrates cenchria*)

The rainbow boa has nine different subspecies, scattered throughout its wide range, in which conditions range from tropical to temperate climates. It is also one of 10 species in the boid genus *Epicrates*, which has members on many West Indian islands, some of which grow almost long enough to be classified as giant snakes. Many of these boas—such as the 13-foot Puerto Rican boa (*E. inoratus*) and the Mona Island boa (*E. monesis*), three feet long and inhabiting only a small island between Puerto Rico and Santo Domingo—are extremely rare. They are also a marvelous example of how a group of animals from a single basic stock can evolve into different species when isolated on islands. The rainbow boa is the only member of its genus in South America. It is hardy and largely a forest species but can make do with many other habitats.

Range: Colombia to Argentina, coast to coast.

Size: Six feet.

Remarks: Often kept in captivity because of its hardiness.

Emerald tree boa (*Corallus caninus*)

This snake belongs to a genus that includes four species of slender boas that live primarily in trees. Like some other snakes, young emerald tree boas differ in color from adults. The young are reddish but turn brilliant green as juveniles. Adults have white cross marks on their backs, helping them blend into the leaves, where they lie in ambush for birds. It consumes its prey while hanging head downwards from a branch. It is primarily a rain forest animal.

Range: Amazon region of South America.

Size: Five to six feet.

Remarks: In captivity, the emerald tree boa will eat rats, although it prefers birds.

Europe (and Western Asia)

FAMILY: COLUBRIDAE

Balkan whip-snake (*Coluber genonensis*)

The long, slender tail of this snake is responsible for its name. It is an active hunter of lizards and sometimes other snakes, nestling birds, and small rodents. Rather than lying in ambush, it swiftly pursues prey. Once contact is made, the whip snake uses its body to pin its victim to the ground, then engulfs it. As suits a snake with this type of hunting behavior, the whip snake is extremely alert, has excellent vision, and is fast moving, even on rugged terrain.

Range: Northern Yugoslavia through Greece and Mediterranean Islands, including Crete.

Size: Usually about three feet, but can reach a length of five feet.

Smooth snake (*Coronella austriaca*)

Like the ubiquitous garter snake is in North America, this species is one of the most widespread and abundant snakes of Europe and adjacent sections of Asia. However, it is not often seen because it likes to burrow into the soil—sandy soil is its preference—and hide under low vegetation. It is particularly common in scrubby vegetation, such as heather.

Aesculapian snake (*Elaphe longissima*)

This is the snake—or two snakes—entwined on the Cadeus staff of Aesculapius, the Romano-Greek god of healing. The staff remains a symbol of medicine today. It is a widespread species of both Europe and western Asia. There are a small number of subspecies, debated by taxonomists, including *persica* in Iran and *romana* in Southern Italy. Olive brown in color, the Aesculapian snake is able to withstand moderately cold weather. It lives up to 5,000 feet in parts of the Alps, although there it is restricted to sheltered, sunny areas. Scientists believe that it may migrate to lower altitudes when it holes up for the winter. Small rodents are the mainstay of this snake's diet. However, it is an adept climber and occasionally feeds on nestling birds.

Range: Much of southern Europe and western Asia, from Spain to Iran, north to southern Russia; also on some of the Greek Islands.

Size: Three to four feet, sometimes approaching six feet.

Remarks: During the mating season, males and females engage in an elaborate courtship ritual, twisting the rear of their bodies together and raising the forebody in an S shape.

Africa

FAMILY: COLUBRIDAE
Slug-eating snake (*Duberria variegata*)

There are two slug-eating snakes in Africa. This species ranges most of the continent. The other species (*D. lutrix*) is confined to the southern portion of the continent. There are many types of small snakes that are secretive, often burrowing, and which feed on slugs and snails. This species is typical. Given the nature of its prey, it is found in moist areas.

Range: Southern Africa to Ethiopia.

Size: About a foot.

Remarks: Hooked teeth enable it to extract a snail from its shell.

Wolf snake (*Lycophidon capense*)

The wolf snake is one of the most widespread non-venomous snakes in Africa. It is primarily a species of open country. Terrestrial, it feeds mainly on small lizards, especially skinks. Long teeth in its jaw—wolf-like teeth give it its name—enable it to grasp its wriggly prey. It is an active hunter, abroad mostly during the day. Its diurnal hunting pattern exposes it to other hunters, birds of prey that feed on snakes. For the wolf snake, a day's survival can be a matter of kill or be killed.

Range: Egypt to the Cape of Good Hope.

Size: Less than three feet at most.

Remarks: Its range largely parallels that of the skinks which are its prey. Taxonomists differ on whether or not, throughout its range, the wolf snake is divided into several species or subspecies.

Cape file snake (*Mehelya capensis*)

Gray to black in color, these snakes feed on other serpents. They are capable of consuming snakes almost as large as they. It appears to be immune to most venoms because it regularly feeds on venomous snakes. This snake lives mainly in open country but can also be found in islands of woodland on plains and savannas.

Range: East Africa to the Cape of Good Hope.

Size: To five feet.

Remarks: The name of this snake comes from the triangular cross section of its body. It is not related to the aquatic file snakes (see below) of Asia.

House snake (*Boaedon lineatum*)

Dark brown to black in color, this small snake is a boon to residents of African villages. It feeds mostly on small rodents, especially rats. Thus, it is drawn to places where rats congregate; human habitations. It has adapted to living in and around structures created by people. It hides in trash heaps and even weaves its way into the thatched roofs that cover many homes in rural Africa. Its penchant for living where people live has given it its name. Indeed, this little snake often enters houses. It is one of the snakes most often encountered by people in its range. The house snake sometimes feeds on small birds as well as rodents. It is an opportunist. Karl P. Schmidt and Robert F. Inger, in their classic book *Living Reptiles of the World*, write of a house snake that entered a canary cage and ate the bird.

Range: Eastern Africa.

Size: Three feet, at most.

Remarks: This snake may climb on to rooftops, but, by nature, it is terrestrial. Other species of house snakes are found on the Arabian Peninsula and the Seychelles islands.

Egg-eating snake (*Dasypeltis scabra*)

The ability of this snake to swallow bird eggs, puncture them in its throat, consume the insides and spit out the shell is well-known. It can engulf an egg the size of the hen's eggs that you keep in the refrigerator, yet its girth is not much larger than a man's finger. Commonly, the egg upon which it feeds can be four times larger than its own head. Egg-eating snakes live largely in open areas, such as savannas, but are also found in lightly forested regions.

Range: Tropical Africa to temperate southern Africa.

Size: Three feet.

Remarks: There are other snakes that feed upon eggs, but they swallow the entire egg and digest the shell as well as the insides. None of these snakes can consume eggs so large relative to their size.

Mole snake (*Pseudodaspis cana*)

Long and thick bodied, this snake is an impressive creature that could cause a scare if encountered in the field. However, it is not venomous. The mole snake feeds mostly on small mammals, especially rodents, although scientists believe that the young may prefer lizards.

Range: Central Africa to Southern Africa.

Size: Almost seven feet.

Remarks: This snake can produce up to 100 live young.

Asia

FAMILY: XENOPELTIDAE

Sunbeam snake (*Xenopeltis unicolor*)

Sunbeam snakes, named for the iridescence of their scales, inhabit both the tropics of America and Asia. This Asian species is brownish in color. Like other sunbeam snakes, it is a burrower, which feeds largely on amphibians, other snakes, small rodents and, sometimes birds. In their book, *Living Reptiles of the World*, famed herpetologists Karl P. Schmidt and Robert E. Inger note that birds taken by the sunbeam snake may be those that have died and fallen to the ground. When alarmed, it acts in the manner of many of the colubrid snakes, vibrating its tail, a behavior that Schmidt and Inger denote as "foreshadowing the development of the rattle of the rattlesnakes."

Range: Southeast Asia.

Size: Up to 40 inches.

Remarks: Taxonomists consider this snake quite primitive.

FAMILY: ACROCHORIDAE

Java wart snake (*Acrochordus javanicus*)

The wart snakes are the most aquatic of all serpents except for the sea snakes. The Java wart snake is best known of this group. This species is virtually helpless on land and apparently never leaves the water. It bears live young—sometimes more than 70 of them—in the water. Like sea snakes, the Java wart snake has a body that is laterally compressed for efficient travel through the aquatic environment. And, like sea snakes but unlike other snakes, the scales of the wart snake do not overlap, a quality that decreases water resistance. The scales of the wart snake, on its loose, wrinkled skin, are rough and granular. The skin of the wart snake was once prized for the snake leather market. Thousands of wart snakes have been killed for this reason.

Wart snakes feed largely on minnows and other small fish. Their dark-brown bodies and the crinkled appearance of their skin serves them as camouflage when they creep into submerged roots and aquatic vegetation of languid rivers. They wait in ambush for prey. Sometimes they grab fish with a fast, side movement of their jaws. Another feeding behavior is especially interesting. Fish that are fooled by the wart snake's camouflage sometimes seek a hiding place among the loose folds of its skin. Observations several years ago at the Bronx Zoo showed that the snake can contract its skin and trap a fish that has sought refuge there.

Range: Southern Asia and East Indies.

Size: Up to six feet.

Remarks: Sometimes called the "elephant-trunk snake" because of its loosely folded skin, or the "file snake" due to its rough scales.

FAMILY: COLUBRIDAE
White-bellied water snake (*Fordonia leucobalia*)

This is a highly unusual snake. It inhabits coastal mudflats and mangrove swamps. Therefore, it is adapted to living in areas flooded by tidal brackish water. Few snakes eat crabs. The white-bellied water snake subsists almost entirely on them. It is the only member of its genus.

Range: Coastal Southeast Asia, the Philippines, New Guinea and northern Australia.

Size: About two feet.

Remarks: Herpetologist Chris Mattison, in his book *The Encyclopedia of Snakes*, notes that this species sometimes eats crabs "piecemeal" which is extraordinary among snakes, who usually devour food whole.

Flying snake (*Chrysopelea ornata*) (also *paradisii*)

The flying snake doesn't really fly; it parachutes. This snake, which lives in the branches of rain forest trees, can invert its belly, making its underside concave. The result is what amounts to an elongated parachute. The "parachute" traps air when the snake decides to travel from the trees to lower branches, slowing its descent.

Range: Southeast Asia.

Size: About four feet.

Remarks: Sometimes called the "ornate flying snake" because of its coloration: green and black with petal-shaped spots on its back.

Australia

FAMILY: TYPHLOPIDAE
Blind snake (*Typhlina nigrescens*)

This species is one of the Australian versions of blind snakes, which are primitive burrowing snakes, yet have colonized more of the world than most other snakes. They feed on termites and ants, even large biting ants. They are common, but not often seen because they spend so much time underground or under debris.

Range: Many different habitats throughout Australia, including woodlands, plains and areas of human habitation.

FAMILY: COLUBRIDAE
Green tree snake (*Dendrelaphis punctulata*)

This snake is very colorful. It is green, with spots of yellow or blue peeking out from beneath its scales. Its bottom is bright yellow. Active by day, the green tree snake dens up in rocky crevices on the ground but often hunts tree frogs in the branches. Still, it is a generalist, as far as feeding habits are concerned. It will eat small rodents, birds and other reptiles.

Range: Temperate Australia, outside of hot deserts.

Size: About two feet.

Remarks: This is a feisty snake that will bite if provoked. Bites cause bleeding, but are not serious.

FAMILY: ELAPIDAE
Krefft's dwarf snake (*Cacophis krefftii*)

This little snake is an example of a small group of Australian elapids that, while technically dangerous, pose no threat to people. The venom of these snakes is barely toxic to humans and, moreover, their teeth lack the size and power to introduce a significant amount of poison. Also, these snakes generally are inoffensive and seldom bite people. The harmless nature of the dwarf snake is evidenced by the fact that it is commonly killed by domestic cats. It feeds almost entirely on skinks.

Range: Much of Australia's forested areas, particularly wet forests around the rim of the continent.

Size: About one foot.

Remarks: This snake is almost entirely nocturnal.

Green tree python (*Chondropython viridi*)

This look-alike for the emerald tree boa of tropical America is a tree snake. It prowls the branches of tropical forests, often lying in ambush for birds. It coils around a branch, with its head hanging down, like a vine. When a bird comes close, the python tries to snatch it up in its jaws. Small birds may be killed on impact. Larger ones are constricted before being swallowed.

Range: Australasia.

Size: No more than five feet.

Remarks: Its shiny green skin makes it one of the world's most beautiful snakes.

CHAPTER 10

Snakes in Our Minds

Ironically, many peoples of developing countries where dangerous snakes abound simply accept them as a fact of life. In some cultures, moreover, snakes are considered a sign of good luck and even are revered. The classical Greeks certainly had a high opinion of snakes. A snake living in a home was thought to bring divine favor, and serpents were a symbol of Asclepius, the Greek god of healing. The caduceus, the staff embraced by two serpents, is still used as the standard of today's medical physician.

Perhaps no other animal has had such a profound impact upon the human psyche as the snake. There is something about the snake that enables it to creep into the human mind and soul as no other animal can. The attitudes of humans towards the snake are remarkably ambivalent, and have been so since at least the dawn of civilization.

Satan Personified

The Biblical account of Genesis certainly gave the snake a bad rap. The nomadic desert Semites who penned the book apparently had contact with venomous snakes, sand vipers and perhaps an occasional cobra. Snakes, in their minds, were dangerous and sly, as was the Devil. "The serpent was more cunning than any beast of the field," said the writers of Genesis. So it was natural that, with their potent use of imagery, the shepherds who wrote Genesis characterized the Tempter of Eve as a serpent. "The serpent deceived me," said Eve, and so she ate the forbidden fruit and, although with Adam, was cast from the Garden of Eden.

In retribution, God cursed the snake and condemned it to living on its belly in dust. And he placed an enmity between the woman and her descendants, and the serpent. Christians interpret the Biblical pronouncement of the Almighty that a male descendent of Eve would crush the snake under his heel as a prophesy of the Christ who was to come.

The Biblical image of the snake as the personification of evil has shaped human antipathy of snakes in Western societies. Many a snake has been killed because of a predisposition on the part of many people to regard serpents as peculiarly sinister. Satan depicted as a snake in the Bible may be a continuation of a tradition from the Sumerian Epic of Gilgamesh, which prefigured several Biblical stories, including that of the Flood. In the epic, the hero Gilgamesh, viewed by the Sumerians as a demigod, possessed a herb that gave him immortality, but lost it to a thieving snake.

Good Snake, Bad Snake

Ironically, the Hebrews, along with many other ancient peoples of the Mediterranean region, also cast the snake in a good light. When Aaron's staff turned into a snake and devoured the snakes that Pharaoh's priests had conjured up from their own staves, it was a case of good snake destroying bad snake. Throughout the Middle East and the Mediterranean in ancient times, snakes were vilified on one hand and glorified on the other. For many cultures, snakes were considered as representing fertility—of the Earth as well as of humans. A figure of the mother goddess worshipped by the Minoans of Crete, dated to 1500 B.C., shows her holding a snake in each hand. Besides its obvious phallic symbolism, the powers of fertility invested in the snake may also have stemmed from the way a serpent sheds its skin, and emerges as a shining new creature, larger than before.

The ancient Egyptians also viewed snakes as both good and bad. Certainly, venomous snakes were a threat to life and limb, especially in pre-dynastic times, when the evolving Egyptians were largely agricultural villagers who were likely to encounter dangerous snakes such as cobras in their day-to-day lives. In his book *Zoo of the Gods*, Anthony S. Mercante notes that inscriptions in Egyptian pyramids contained many prayers by worshippers asking to be protected from snakebite. Mercante describes an Egyptian belief that the evil serpent Apet tried to prevent the sun diety Ammon-Ra from rising each morning. Priests of the sun god figured a way out of the problem. They made a wax image of a snake, inscribed with the name of Apet, and burned it. Apparently, the ceremony worked; the sun came up every morning. Due to the way the snake emerges from its shed skin, the Egyptians also considered the serpent as a symbol of fertility and rebirth. In effect, when it came to the snake, the Egyptians had it both ways.

The Greeks of both the Bronze Age and the Classical Period that followed were particularly ambivalent about snakes. For the Greeks—and the Romans who adopted their religion and legends—there really were good snakes and bad snakes. Whether a snake was good or bad sometimes depended on one's viewpoint. Legend has it that when the Greeks who had been besieging Troy left their wooden horse hehind, a Trojan priest, Laocoon, warned his countrymen to beware of Greeks bearing gifts. Two giant serpents, sent by the goddess Athena, who sided with the Greeks, promptly emerged from the sea, wrapped the priest, as well as his two sons, in its coils and killed them. Hercules often battled giant snakes that belonged to one god or another.

The tales of huge constricting snakes in Greek legends make one wonder. Did these ancients know about the giant pythons of Africa and Asia? Was it a racial memory? At any rate, the name "Python" itself is Greek. Python was a giant snake that lived in a cave on Mount Parnassus, at Delphi. Apollo destroyed it with his arrows. Legend gives various reasons for why he did it. One was that Python had guarded the oracle there, but afterwards, the oracle was dedicated to Apollo. The god Apollo apparently took over Python's turf. The roots of this story are lost in the past, but it may tell of a battle between two cults.

In Greek legend, snakes could be bad customers, indeed. They formed the hair of the Gorgon Medusa, slain by Perseus; and of the furies, all of which were deadly to men. Even so, the ancient Greeks also viewed serpents as a symbol of healing. Asclepius, reputed to be the son of Apollo and a maiden that he favored, was revered as the father of healing. Some accounts say that he learned his skills from the legendary Chiron, the centaur. Other tales tell that he watched snakes, healing one another with herbs. Not inconceivably, the father of physicians used snake venom, commonly utilized in traditional Asian medicine, to treat illnesses.

In many Asian cities, such as Hong Kong, there are streets lined with markets selling snakes and snake products for medicinal purposes. Many, if not most, of the serpents offered for sale are venomous species. Hanging from hooks outside these shops are the bodies of kraits and sea snakes, side by side in neat alignment. Inside the shops are shelves stocked with medicinal preparations of snake products, including gall bladders and fat. Snake products—indeed, many animal products—are important ingredients in Asian medicine, used to treat problems ranging from rheumatism to tuberculosis. Western medicine has long looked upon many of the Asian medical practices as superstitions, but increasingly, as the growing use of acupuncture demonstrates, physicians of the West are looking with interest upon the healing methods of the East. Snake venoms are today under investigation by western researchers as a possible treatment for stroke. One way or the other, snakes, as noted earlier, became the symbol of the great healer, as they still are emblematic of medicine today. People who hate snakes or have phobias about them, seldom realize that the physicians who are treating them consider a staff with entwined snakes as their symbol.

166

SNAKE FABLES

Religious beliefs aside, there exists a host of tall tales about snakes, some of which are still considered as gospel by many people. Here is the fact and fiction about some of them:

- *Horsehair scattered around a campsite is a barrier to rattlers. (It does not work, just a superstition from the Old West.)*
- *Snakes use their eyes and sinuous body movements to enchant prey, especially birds. (Not true, but some small creatures may freeze at the approach of a predator.)*
- *Milk snakes drain milk from the udders of cows. (No. They merely prowl around barns in search of rodents.)*
- *Mother snakes swallow their young to protect them. (To the contrary, many snakes eat young of their own species as well as other species.)*
- *Some snakes take tail in mouth and form a hoop, to roll away from danger. (Old cowboy fallacy.)*

Take Up Serpents

Given the hold that snakes have on the human imagination, it is not surprising that, virtually around the world, there are myriad cults in which snakes are used in religious rituals. These sects range from African tribes that revere the rock python to Christian sects in the rural southern Appalachians that handle rattlesnakes to test their faith in the Almighty. If a snake handler is bitten and sickened or, worse yet, dies, the disaster is attributed to a lack of faith. These rituals are based upon a passage in the Gospel of St. Mark that states, "In my name . . . they shall take up serpents . . . it shall not hurt them." The snake most often used in these ceremonies is the timber rattlesnake. The relatively passive nature of this species doubtless contributes to the infrequency of bites to the believers who handle them. So, perhaps, does the expertise of the handlers. The fact that venomous snakes often bite defensively without delivering a dose of their poison also is a boost to the belief in divine protection.

One of the most famous snake rituals is the Snake Dance performed by secret societies of the Hopi Indians in the American Southwest. The motive behind the dance, which in itself is not performed in secret but is often a tourist attraction, is to bring down the rains. Hopi Snake priests dance while holding serpents, including dangerous rattlesnakes, both in their hands and clenched between their jaws. For years, herpetologists have debated whether or not the priests handle rattlers whose fangs have been removed or those with fangs that are fully functional. An old acquaintance of mine, Charles M. Bogert, who was chairman of the department of amphibians and reptiles at the American Museum of Natural History, surreptitiously examined one of the ceremonial rattlesnakes in the 1930s. He found that, indeed, its fangs had been cut out. This is not to say that all rattlesnakes used in the dance are in that condition. Some may well be in full possession of their venom apparatus. The Snake priests are expert snake handlers. Whatever the truth of the matter, the Hopis are not telling.

The idea of snakes as bringers of rain is found in many human cultures. As Chris Mattison notes in his book *The Encyclopedia of Snakes,* many peoples have looked to snakes as water givers. These beliefs may be due to the fact that during dry periods, snakes hole up underground to conserve moisture, but appear on the surface when the rains come.

Australian Aboriginal lore is full of references to snakes and the rains. During the dry season, the "rainbow snakes," prominent in the complex art of the native Australians, are believed to live at the bottoms of "permanent waterholes," says Mattison. When the rains arrive, the rainbow snakes soar into the skies.

In my living room is a wooden carving, crafted by an artisan in a small village on the banks of the Zambezi River on the eastern border of Zimbabwe. The region there is dry, with sandy soil studded by thorny acacia trees. The borders of the river are flood plains, verdant during high water, bone dry when the rains are late. According to local tradition, the rains come or go because of the reptilian river deity imaged in the carving that I brought home. It represents *Nyami nyami,* river god of the Zambezi. The carving is indisputably serpentine. It rises from a coiled, scaled body. Its head is massive, with open jaws, like those of a python, although its teeth suggest those of a hippo. Who—or what—is this diety? Along the Zambezi, the people say that when *Nyami nyami* rises from the depths of the broad river and mates with his female counterpart, the rains come.

Snake Charmers

Perhaps the best-known of snake handlers are the snake charmers of India—there are snake charmers in Africa as well. These men earn a living by allegedly charming venomous snakes, particularly cobras, into harmlessness via music from a flute. The cobra rears up and spreads its hood, then sways to and fro. As with the Hopi priests, there are suspicions that the cobras have been tampered with by fang removal or venom milking. But make no mistake about it, many professional snake charmers are experts on the behavior of snakes and how to use it to their advantage. They try to stay just out of range of the cobra's strike, which in any event is slow compared to that of, for example, a rattlesnake. As for the music of the flute, it matters not at all. Snakes cannot hear it. The ability of the charmer to transfix the snake's attention is caused by movements of the flute and the charmer's body in front of the snake.

Roy Pinney, a former professor at the University of Alaska and a television producer, photographer and writer, wrote extensively about snake charmers in his 1981 book, *The Snake Book.* He claimed that Indian snake charmers are members of a "closed society." The technique of charming snakes is passed from father to son. Most snake charmers, says Pinney, begin training as children. It is virtually a male occupation. Pinney opines that despite their expertise, some snake charmers are indeed envenomated and even killed by cobras. "Indeed," he wrote, "the mortality rate is rather high among snake charmers."

The Feathered Serpent

One snake cult may have helped lead to the downfall of Mexico's Aztec empire. Despite the fact that they regularly sacrificed people to a host of bloody gods, the Aztecs also revered the divinity Quetzalcoatl, who was symbolized by a feathered, or plumed, serpent. The cult of the feathered serpent was a tradition that the Aztecs inherited from Meso-American cultures that preceded them, notably the Toltecs. According to legend, Quetzalcoatl arrived from who knows where and ushered in a period of peace and prosperity in land that before him was wracked by war. Although he was depicted as a feathered serpent, legend also had it he was a tall, fair-skinned man. An unknown turn of events, perhaps a political coup, forced the feathered serpent to depart, on what sounds suspiciously like a sailing vessel. Was the feathered serpent a Viking, who traveled on a ship with a prow shaped like a dragon's head? It is an interesting speculation. At any rate, when Cortez and his Spaniards arrived in Mexico, with the white sails of their vessels billowing in the wind, and their white skins, the Aztecs at first suspected he was the feathered serpent returning. They let their guard down, allowing the invader to gain the upper hand and eventually destroy their civilization.

The Real Snake

The snake in nature can be quite different from the one in our minds. Snakes are not sinister, nor are they cunning. Their brains are primitive, at least compared to those of birds and mammals. They simply go about their business in the fashion in which they have evolved: and their business is both individual survival and procreating their individual species. Their true wonder is not based on the mystical or supernatural. They are in themselves, with their remarkable adaptations, wondrous creatures.

The Conservation of Snakes

Snakes are subject to the same stresses on the environment experienced by other animals. Some of these stresses are natural, like drought and volcanic eruptions. However, snakes have been able to deal with these pressures for millions of years and still survive. The environmental degradation caused by humans is another matter. Many species of snakes, which are equipped to counter the vagaries of nature, are declining in numbers. Many have dwindled to the point that they are in danger of extinction. Others, while not endangered as a species, are disappearing regionally. The main reason for the decline, as it is for most other imperiled types of animals, is destruction of habitat and other disruptions of the snake's natural world by human activities.

Causes of Decline

The environmental crunch caused by humans becomes worse for an animal if it has highly specialized or restricted habitat requirements. Island snakes are particularly at risk. The genus of boas called *Epicrates* is a prime example. Almost a half dozen members of this genus evolved into separate species on various Caribbean islands, such as Puerto Rico and Jamaica. Some of them, such as the Puerto Rican boa, which reaches a length of more than 12 feet, almost qualify as giant snakes. By and large, these are forest snakes, which feed on birds and small mammals. There is precious little tropical forest left on any of the islands that these snakes inhabit. People have seen to that. Puerto Rico, for example, was once covered by tropical forest. Today, only fragments of forest remain, mostly under the care of the United States Forest Service. Individual boas can eke out survival in these sanctuaries but, as a species, they are imprisoned. Outside of guarded forests, they have no place to live. If a natural disaster such as a hurricane disrupts the forest, destroying cover and the prey upon which they feed, the boas are especially vulnerable. They have no other place to go on the island—the concrete streets of San Juan are no option—much less get off the island. Virtually all of the boas of the West Indies are in danger of extinction.

Even species of snakes living on continental land masses, if they have been confined to small areas of habitat, can be pushed to extinction's brink by the same forces that threaten island animals. The San Francisco garter snake is one of the rarest snakes in the United States. It never had a wide range—mainly San Mateo County on the San Francisco Peninsula, but was abundant within those boundaries. This brightly colored snake provides an excellent example of how many factors, ranging from natural restrictions to human interference, can cause a snake, or any animal, to slide towards extinction. A limited geographical range is one; that is one strike against the San Francisco garter snake. Another is specialization for a certain type of habitat. The San Francisco garter snake is found in wetlands, near streams, and around ponds. It feeds largely on amphibians, such as the red-legged frog and newts. Most of its former habitat has been destroyed by development, including housing tracts, channeling of rivers and road construction. Development is strike two. Strike three is the bullfrog. This species, the largest frog in North America, has been introduced into the snake's habitat. Voracious, it feeds largely on the frogs that are the garter snake's diet, and perhaps even on the garter snakes themselves. Efforts to preserve this snake have been minimal. Only a handful of state and county preserves are maintained for use as management areas for the snake.

Another threat to the San Francisco garter snake is illegal collecting. It is a species protected by both state and federal law, but some snake fanciers continue to gather it from the wild, despite the threat of arrest. Collecting snakes, either for the pet trade or for their skins, is a major cause of the decline of many species. The impact of collecting is vastly increased when a species already has been decimated by pressures such as habitat loss. The massive Indian python is one such species. Wild lands in India are scarce, due to that nation's exploding human population. Forests, the python's main habitat, have been reduced to scraps. Even when the python's habitat was more widespread, and it was relatively abundant, it was mercilessly exploited.

Snake skins have long been a popular source of leather for fashion accessories, ranging from boots to purses, in the western world. Vast numbers of Indian pythons, as well as other pythons and, indeed, many other species of snakes, have been killed for their skins. Chris Mattison, in his book *The Encyclopedia of Snakes*, notes that in 1992, 58,000 Indian python skins were imported into Britain alone. Overall, during the twentieth century, millions upon millions of snakes, mostly from Asia but also from other parts of the world, have been taken from the wild and killed for their skins.

Snake blood, flesh, and other body parts are key ingredients in some remedies of Asian medicine; snake flesh was eaten as a preventative of tubercolosis; and sea snakes were believed to work against malaria and epilepsy. Mattison also reports that snake skins and gall bladders have been used to facilitate childbirth.

Commerce in imperiled snakes—and, for that matter, hundreds of other species—is now controlled by both national and international regulations. However, the rules are far from perfect, and loopholes exist. Poaching and illegal trade persist.

CITES

The most powerful legal instrument in the battle to prevent over-exploitation of snakes—and other animals and plants—

is an international agreement known as CITES, The Convention on International Trade in Endangered Species of Wild Fauna and Flora. It is an international treaty that more than 150 nations have signed. Originated in 1973, it is designed to regulate, and in many cases restrict, international commerce in imperiled animals and plants. The object of CITES is to confirm that trade in imperiled wildlife and plants is legal and does not threaten their survival in the wild. CITES covers not only live organisms, but also their products and products made from those parts. CITES has contributed immensely to the conservation of rare species. However, it is not foolproof. Many nations lack the law enforcement and bureaucratic infrastructure, or the will, to fully police the rules of the treaty. Corruption on the part of government officials also is a problem for CITES. Moreover, there is considerable bickering among treaty signatories about how tightly various species should be regulated. Even so, without CITES, commerce in rare animals would run amuck. With all its faults, it is the most powerful example of how nations can work together for conservation.

CITES groups species under three appendices, according to how imperiled they are:

- *Appendix I contains a list of species that are literally near or on the brink of extinction, either throughout its range or in certain countries. Commercial trade is not permitted in these species. However, individuals of species used for critical scientific research or conservation, usually for the benefit of the species, may be shipped internationally, with strictly scrutinized permits issued by both exporting and important countries.*
- *Appendix II contains a list of species that could be imperiled unless trade is tightly regulated. An importing country must be provided with an export permit from the nation of origin in order to allow a commercial transaction.*
- *Appendix III covers species that are not endangered as a whole, but are subject to intensive conservation programs within individual countries, where these species are dwindling. Trade in these species is regulated by permits and other documents listing the point of origin, so it can be determined whether or not they come from a highly managed population.*

CITES Listing of Snakes

This listing gives the names of snakes covered by CITES, the appendix under which they are listed and, under appendix III, the nations covered. In some cases, only the name of the genus is used because more than one subspecies is endangered. Listing is alphabetical. Family names are in roman type, genus and species are in italics. The list has been slightly modified for the layperson.

Species	Common Name	Appendix
Acrantophis	Madagascar boas	I
Agkistrodon blineatus	cantil	III Honduras
Arteium *schistosum*	olive keelback water snake	III India
Boa constrictor	boa constrictor	II
Boa constrictor occidentalis	Argentine boa constrictor	I
Boidae (all boa constrictors and pythons not specifically listed)		II
Boleria multocarinata	Round Island boa	I
Bothrops asper	terciopelio	III Honduras
Bothrops nasutus	rainforest hog-nosed pit viper	III Honduras
Bothrops nummifer	jumping pit viper	III Honduras
Bothrops ophyomegas	slender hog-nosed pit viper	III Honduras
Bothrops schlegelli	eyelash palm pit viper	
Casarea dussumeriei	Round Island boa	I
Cerberus rhynchops	dog-faced water snake	III India
Clelia clelia	mussurana snake	II
Crotalus durissus	neotropical rattlesnake	III Honduras
Cyclagras gigas	South American false water cobra	II
Elachistodon westermanni	Indian egg-eating snake	II
Epicrates cenchria	rainbow boa	II
Epicrates inoratus	Puerto Rican boa	I
Epicrates monensis	Mona boa	I
Epicrates subflavus	Jamaican boa	I
Eunectes notaeus	yellow anaconda	II

Species	Common Name	Appendix
Hoplocephalus bungaroides	broad-headed snake	II
Micurus diastema	Atlantic coral snake	III Honduras
Micrurus nigrocinctus	black-banded coral snake	III Honduras
Naja naja	Asian (Indian) cobra	II
Ophiophagus hannah	king cobra	II
Ptyas mucosus	oriental rat snake	II
Python (except for the Indian subspecies listed below)		II
Python molurus molurus	Indian python	I
Sanzinia madagascariensis	tree boa	I
Vipera russelii	Russell's viper	III (India)
Vipera ursinii	Orsini's viper	I (Except populations in the former USSR)
Vipera wagneri	Wagner's viper	II
Xenochrophis (Natrix) piscator	checkered keelback water snake	III India

Other Forms of Protection

In addition to CITES, there are other regulations and laws that protect imperiled species. The United States has the Federal Endangered Species Act, which not only protects organisms but the habitat that is critical to their survival. Species that are covered by the act are grouped under two categories. "Endangered" species are those in immediate danger of extinction. "Threatened" species are those that are likely to become extinct without proper management and protection. States have their own endangered species acts as well. Federal and state laws act in concert to protect species in danger. The timber rattlesnake, for example, is not considered by the federal government as endangered or threatened throughout its range. But it is endangered or threatened in many states. Several such states, including Connecticut, Massachusetts and New York, have protected this species under their own endangered species laws.

A solid example of how a state can work to protect a species considered imperiled within its boundaries happened during 1999, in New York. According to a press release issued by the office of the state's Attorney General, Eliot Spencer, here is what happened.

A rock-quarrying company in Dutchess County, about 60 miles up the Hudson from New York City, installed a snake-proof fence around one of its operations. The fence prevented some 20 timber rattlesnakes, which had a den in a nearby state park, from roaming the quarry, a key portion of their habitat. Timber rattlesnakes are considered threatened in New York. The state Department of Environmental Protection went to court to stop the fencing project. A county judge ordered the company to cease building the fence, located less than 300 feet from the den.

Saving Snakes

Saving a snake—or any other animal—from extinction can require a many-pronged approach, because often the threats to the species are multiple and complex. The Antiguan racer is one of the world's most endangered snakes, probably numbering less than 150 adults. It was once common throughout the Caribbean island of Antigua, but is no longer found there due to a series of events. Long ago, the mongoose was introduced into the island to destroy European rats, which in turn had been introduced there accidentally from ships. Mongooses killed rats but, being snake eaters, they also eliminated the racer. The only place where this species survives is on Great Bird Island, about two miles from the coast of Antigua. Mongooses are not present on this islet. However, black rats, which had stowed away on boats that moored near the island, found a home there. The rats preyed upon young racers, so that the population was reduced to about 50 individuals. In 1996, a coalition of conservation groups working with the Antiguan government mounted an intensive campaign against the rats that eliminated them. Scientists closely observed the racers, learning about their life style, especially their breeding habits. A few racers of both sexes were collected and sent to captive breeding facilities operated by the Jersey Wildlife Preservation Trust in the United Kingdom. The racers have produced young and, eventually, there are plans for racers to be released on to other islets off Antigua that are free of both rats and moongooses.

What Good Are Snakes?

The answer to the question is simple. Like all other forms of life, snakes are part of the ecological network that enables life on our planet to function. It is often difficult to predict the impact of the extinction of a species on the living environment. Extinction, after all, is intrinsic to nature. All species are destined to fall over the brink although, before they do, they may give rise to others. When extinction is hastened by the actions of humans, the results may scramble the network. By way of example, cobras kill people. But rats that carry plague and other diseases have been responsible for more human deaths than could ever be attributed to cobras. Rats certainly have their place in the network. So do cobras. Without cobras, the areas in which these snakes live would be overrun by rats. This example may be simplistic. Yet, it has profound implications. Snakes, venomous or harmless, are part of what makes our world tick. Beyond that, they are an intrinsic part of nature's glory.

APPENDIX I

Snakes in the House

Even if you think snakes are loveable, you may not want to have one roaming freely about your house. Snakes occasionally enter dwellings, sometimes in search of rodents and other prey, sometimes in search of shelter, but also by accident. Unless a snake is in a rock cellar, perhaps with a dirt floor, it cannot survive for long within a house. Removing the snake does it a favor. The most common snakes that enter buildings include the black rat snake, the milk snake, the ringneck snake, and garter snakes. All are harmless. If you find a snake in your home, however, be careful. Even in areas where venomous snakes are common, the odds are that the snake in the basement or the wall is harmless. Still, if you have the slightest doubt, contact your local animal control agency, the police, or your state wildlife agency.

Ridding the house of a snake is no easy task. You will probably have to wait it out. The chances of catching it are akin to winning a major lottery. If you do try to grab a snake, wear work gloves because even non-venomous snakes can bite. Some state wildlife agencies suggest that snakes can be lured out of hiding by the warmth of a heating pad or sunlamp focused on a damp towel. If you take this course of action, remember a fire hazard could be involved.

If you have a serious problem with snakes entering your home, you can take protective measures.

- *Seal openings and cracks on the outside of the house and, especially, under doors.*
- *Keep the outside of the house neat and clean. Foundation plantings and stacks of firewood close to the house provide cover for snakes.*
- *Keep the house free of rodents (a good idea even if you are not trying to prevent the entrance of snakes).*
- *If you suspect that a snake is lurking in a particular area, mothballs may drive it away.*

Snakes as Pets

Many people who are interested in snakes keep them as pets. If you are so inclined, here are some suggestions:

- Do not take snakes from the wild.

- Purchase snakes only from a reputable dealer who trades in captive-bred snakes.

- Make sure that the snake is not a protected species. If it is, you probably need a permit or you may not keep it at all.

- Only experienced experts should keep dangerous snakes and, even then, for a purpose, such as scientific research or conservation programs.

- Consider the ramifications of keeping a snake. Some will accept only live food, such as rats and mice. Can you provide?

- Snakes have long life spans. A boa constrictor can live for 20 years—and grow to massive size. Can you handle that?

- Check out a snake's health before purchasing. Dull eyes and scales are often signs of ill health. Consider that if your snake becomes ill, you may have to force-feed it.

- Ahead of time, locate professional help in case your snake sickens. Most veterinarians are not skilled at treating snakes, if they even will.

- Know that you must have a cage that is totally escape proof. It must also have adequate heat and lighting. In the past, people who kept snakes as pets often relied on light bulbs for heat. Now, experienced snake keepers realize that snakes, like other creatures, need a day-night cycle. The lights must go off at some point. So alternative heating is required.

- Cleanup time. If you have a snake as a pet, remember that you cannot walk it to do the doo. You have to clean it from the cage. The floor of the cage should be covered with a substrate that allows easy cleaning; newspapers, for example.

The bottom line is that if you want to keep a snake as a pet, which can be quite rewarding, there is considerable research to do.

BIBLIOGRAPHY

Behler, John L. and King, F. Wayne. 1979. *The Audubon Society Field Guide to North American Reptiles and Amphibians*. New York. Alfred A. Knopf.

Caras, Roger. 1974. *Venomous Animals of the World*. Englewood Cliffs, New Jersey. Prentice-Hall, Inc.

Castellano, Christina. Summer 1997. *Rep Tales*. Bronx, New York. Wildlife Conservation Society.

Conant, Roger. 1958. *A Field Guide to Reptiles and Amphibians*. Boston. Houghton Mifflin Company.

Fritts, Thomas H. 1999. *The Brown Tree Snake: A Fact Sheet for Pacific Island Residents and Travelers*. USGS.

Greene, Harry W. 1997. *Snakes, The Evolution of Mystery in Nature*. London, England. University of California Press.

Harrison, Hal H. 1971. *The World of the Snake*. Philadelphia and New York. J. B. Lippincott Company.

Hollander, Paul. *Care Sheet for Snakes*. pholland@iastate.edu.

Keiser, Edmund D. 1971. *The Poisonous Snakes of Louisiana and the Emergency Treatment of Their Bites*. New Orleans, LA. Louisiana Wild Life and Fisheries Commission.

Klemens, Michael W. 1993. *Amphibians and Reptiles of Connecticut and Adjacent Regions*. Hartford, CT. State Geological and Natural History Survey of Connecticut.

Mattison, Chris. 1995. *The Encyclopedia of Snakes*. New York. Facts on File.

Mercante, Anthony S. *Zoo of the Gods*. 1974. New York, Harper & Row.

Minton, Sherman A, Jr. and Minton, Madge Rutherford. 1969. *Venomous Reptiles*. New York. Charles Scribner's Sons.

Oliver, James A. Personal communications on giant snakes.

———1958. *Snakes in Fact and Fiction*. New York. The MacMillan Company.

———1956. Letter from Dr. Henk Cruys, French Guiana to Dr. Oliver.

Petersen, Richard C. 1970. *Connecticut's Venomous Snakes*. Hartford, CT. State Geological and Natural History Survey of Connecticut.

Pinney, Roy. 1981. *The Snake Book*. Doubleday & Company. Garden City, NY.

Poisonous Snakes of the World. A Manual for Use by U.S. Amphibious Forces. 1966. Washington, DC. Department of the Navy Bureau of Medicine and Surgery.

Pope, Clifford H. 1946. *Snakes of the Northeastern States*. New York. New York Zoological Society.

Ricciuti, Edward R. 1984. *Jungle Animals*. New York. Merigold Press.

———1976. *Killer Animals*. New York. Walker and Company.

———1973. *Killers of the Seas*. New York. Walker and Company.

———1993. *Reptiles*. Woodbridge, CT. Blackbirch Press.

Schmidt, Karl P. and Inger, Robert F. 1957. *Living Reptiles of the World*. Garden City, New York. Doubleday & Company (Hanover House).

Shiels, Andre L. and Bryan, Kelly L. 1998. *Snakes in Basements and Buildings*. Pennsylvania Fish and Boat Commission Press release.

University of Massachusetts, *Snakes and People*. 1996. U.S. Department of Agriculture, Massachusetts Division of Fisheries and Wildlife, UMass Extension.

Spitzer and DEC Win Court Order for Threatened Snakes. 1999. New York State Department of Law. Press release.

Stebbins, Robert C. 1966. *A Field Guide to Western Reptiles and Amphibians*. Boston. Houghton Mifflin Company.

Steward, J.W. 1971. Fairleigh Dickinson University Press, Madison, NJ.

U.S. Government Printing Office. 1999. *Cites Appendices I, II, and III to Convention on International Trade in Endangered Species of Wild Fauna and Flora.*

Wright, Albert Hazen and Wright, Anna Allen. 1957. *Handbook of Snakes, Vol. II.* Ithaca, New York. Comstock Publishing Associates.

Zug, George R. 1993. *Herpetology.* San Diego. Academic Press.

INDEX